Living LANGUAGE

LANGUAGE, POWER AND IDENTITY

Michael Butler
and
George Keith

Hodder & Stoughton

A MEMBER OF THE HODDER HEADLINE GROUP

Acknowledgements

The publishers would like to thank the following for their kind permission to reproduce copyright material:

Text 2 from the *Lexicon of Contemporary English* © Longman; Text 3 from *Roget's Thesaurus*; Text 7 © The Stationery Office; Text 11 'Mad dogs and Englishmen', as appeared in the *Guardian*, 23 January 1991, © *Guardian Newspapers*; Text 13 © *Kellogs*'; Text 14 reproduced with permission of the *Observer*, as appeared in the *Observer*, 18 February 1996; Text 15 reproduced with permission of the *Observer*, as appeared in the *Observer*, 7 April 1996; Text 19 from *In Search of Excellence* by Thomas J. Peters and Robert H. Waterman Jr, reproduced with permission of HarperCollins; Text 20 from *Organisational Behaviour* by Andrzej Huczynski and David Buchanan, reproduced with permission of Prentice Hall; Text 21 from *Trainspotting* © Irvine Welsh; Text 22 © *Radio Times*; Text 23 'Whose News do you Use' by Steve Clarke reproduced with permission of *Radio Times*; Text 24 'Television Hits the Dumber Switch' by Ferdinand Mount, first appeared in *The Sunday Times*, 2 February 1998, © News International; Text 25 'Seeming is Believing' by Ian Parker © the *Independent*; Text 26 'Spin doctors furious . . .' by Kamal Ahmed and Anne Perkins from the *Guardian*, 2 July 1998, reproduced with permission from *Guardian Newspapers*; Text 27 'Arts Council sidelines . . .' by John Harlow, from *The Sunday Times*, 8 February 1998, © *News International*; Text 30 © Deborah Cameron; Text 32a and Text 32b © *News International*; Text 33 'Rebel MP attacks Blair's Stepford Wives' by John Hibbs published 7 February 1998 in the *Daily Telegraph* © Telegraph Group Limited, London, 1998; Text 36 © Andrew Duncan, *Radio Times*; Text 38 © 1997 *The Spice Girls*; Text 40 'The problem with Girl Power' by Beatrix Campbell from the *Guardian*, 11 November 1997; Text 41 'The Unknown Citizen' by W H Auden reprinted from *Collected Shorter Poems 1927–57* with permission from *Faber and Faber Ltd*; Text 44 reproduced with permission from *The Labour Party*; Text 48 reproduced with permission from *The Body Shop*; Text 58 'Moral Crusade Gathers Pace' by Ewen MacAskill and John Carvell reproduced with permission of *Guardian Newspapers*.

Every effort has been made to trace copyright holders of material reproduced in this book. Any rights not acknowledged will be acknowledged in subsequent printings if notice is given to the publisher.

Orders: please contact Bookpoint Ltd, 39 Milton Park, Abingdon, Oxon OX14 4TD. Telephone: (44) 01235 400414, Fax: (44) 01235 400454. Lines are open from 9.00 – 6.00, Monday to Saturday, wtih a 24 hour message answering service. Email address: orders@bookpoint.co.uk

British Library Cataloguing in Publication Data
A catalogue record for this title is available from The British Library

ISBN 0 340 73085 4

First published 1999

Impression number 10 9 8 7 6 5 4 3 2 1
Year 2005 2004 2003 2002 2001 2000 1999

Cover photo from The Ronald Grant Archive
Typeset by Fakenham Photosetting Limited, Fakenham, Norfolk NR21 8NL
Printed in Great Britain for Hodder & Stoughton Educational, a division of Hodder Headline Plc, 338 Euston Road, London NW1 3BH by Scotprint Ltd, Musselburgh, Scotland.

Contents

The Purpose of this Book

This book is chiefly concerned with how different kinds of social power are encoded and expressed in written texts. It is a big topic that covers many aspects of modern life:

- health
- social services
- big business
- advertising.
- communication media
- gender representations
- different lifestyles

The main focus throughout the book is on texts, and the aim of the book is to show you how texts may be investigated.

You will find many texts in the chapters of this book but it is important, right from the start, that you collect similar texts you have discovered in magazines, leaflets, books and on the Internet. Investigate these along the lines we demonstrate.

Investigation requires some guiding ideas and some sort of method. Above all, method should act as a useful support, and not become a straitjacket. 'Language and Power' is an easy topic to get lost in, and it is method that saves you from losing your bearings. Below we have set out an overview of the methodological approach adopted in this book. Do not try to learn it in one go; have a look at the way it is organised and then move on to Chapter One. Every so often you will find it useful to refer back to this section, and gradually you will find that you have assimilated its four guiding ideas and the twelve questions you will most frequently need to ask.

The aim of investigation is to make connections between the language in the text (lexis and grammar) and the big issues that lie behind texts.

Behind the text

1 What is the world view, ideology, belief and value system lying behind the text? This is often implied or taken for granted, for example, the party political allegiance of newspapers.

2 Are there any contradictory ideas or values behind or underlying the text? A censorious moral attitude mixed with sensationalist enjoyment, for example, can be seen in many front page newspaper stories.

3 What point of view, ideology, beliefs do you, the reader, bring to the text?

These are all *macro* level questions.

Making connections between the language in the text and the big issues that lie behind texts

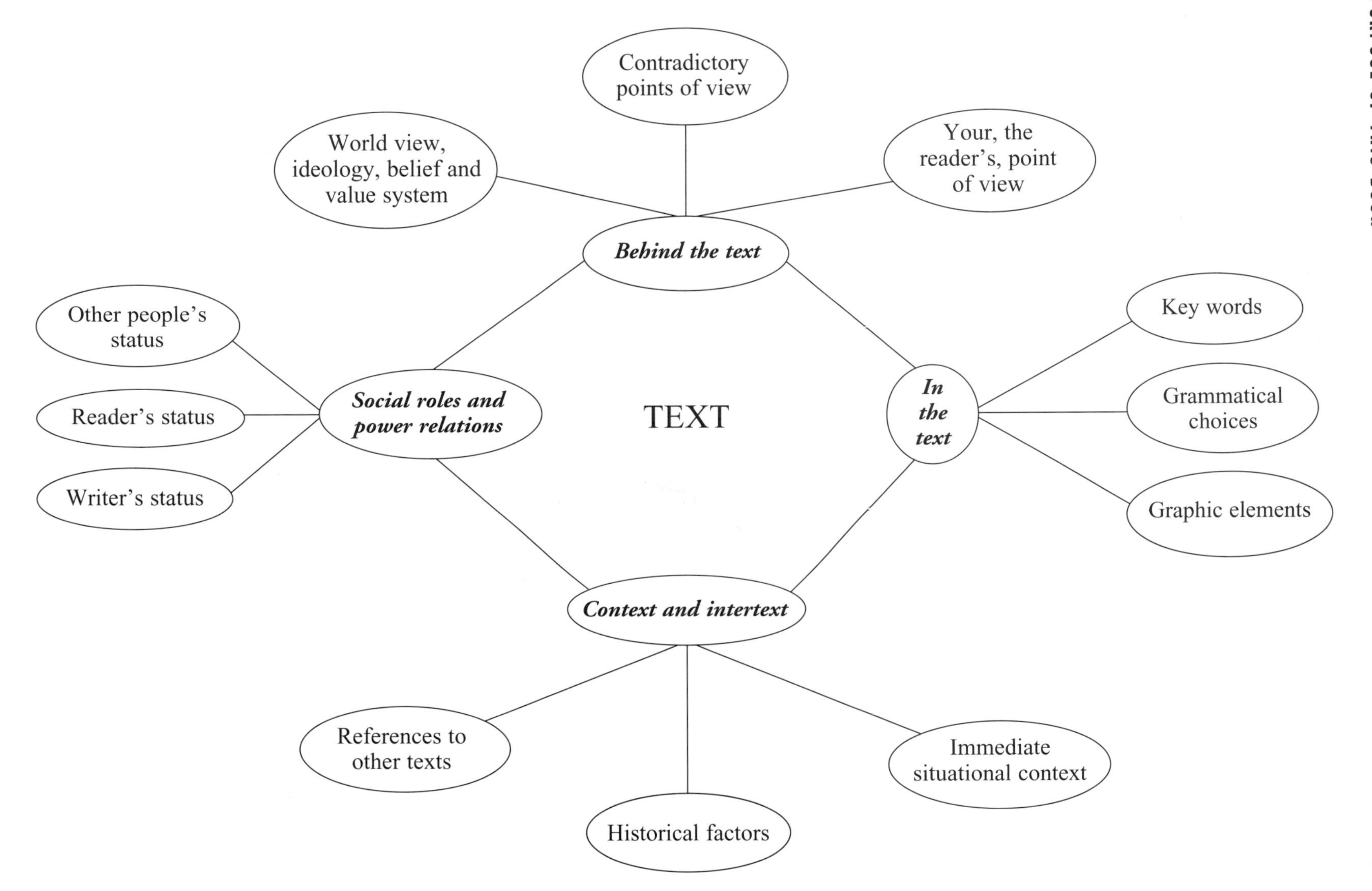

In the text

4 What 'key words' are there in the text? These might be distinctive lexical choices, semantic fields, specialist vocabulary, euphemisms, antonyms and synonyms and metaphors.

5 What grammatical choices have been made? Look at sentence function, modality, passivisation, pronoun reference.

6 What graphic elements (pictures, typography) contribute to the meaning of the text?

These are all *micro* level approaches that help to explain the macro ideas.

Context and intertext

7 What is the immediate situational context? Think about overt purpose, intended audience, point of writer/reader contact.

8 What historical factors contribute to the text? These might include prior knowledge and experience, connotations in words, interpretative slant on events, people and 'things' in the text, age of the text.

9 What references are made to other texts in the culture? These need not be written texts; they could be film, song, TV.

These are a mixture of *micro* and *macro* level observations.

Social roles and power relations

10 What is the status and assumed or adopted role of the writer(s)? Authoritative/authoritarian? Egalitarian? Legal?

11 What role is assigned to the reader? This is sometimes explicit, but is often implicit. It may be welcomed or resented but is frequently unnoticed and, therefore, complied with.

12 What roles are assigned to persons in the text itself? Who is proactive? reactive? inert? passively acquiescent?

These are macro questions but, again, the answers will lie in the micro evidence.

All the texts in this book will be approached by various combinations of these questions. Each text will represent a particular kind of **discourse**, that is to say, a particular way of addressing, communicating with, talking to people about a particular topic or activity. **Stylistics** is a way of describing discourse by showing how meanings are constructed through uses of lexis, grammar and phonology.

1 The Idea of Power

In this chapter you will:

- identify different fields of study in the topic 'Language and Society', one of which is the relationship between power and language
- explore your own and dictionary meanings of 'power'
- investigate aspects of power as revealed in selected texts
- practise your own power as a critical reader.

Language and society

Language is everywhere in society. The two words are almost one and the same thing. In A-Level syllabuses, under the general heading of 'Language and Society', the word 'language' pairs conveniently with a number of other concepts: 'language and gender', 'language and social class', 'language and education', 'language and the media'. In recent years 'language and power' has become a very popular 'Language and Society' topic, equal in significance to 'language and class' and 'language and gender'. Some would go so far as to argue that issues of social class and gender are essentially issues of power.

Before considering power, it will help to get a perspective on this huge syllabus area called 'Language and Society'. You can do this by identifying four aspects:

1. **Purpose** – language is used to achieve purposes which can be classified in all sorts of ways, for example, to enquire, persuade, inform, entertain, instruct, frighten and reassure.
2. **Addresser/Addressee** (sometimes referred to as audience) – somebody somewhere is communicating with someone, directly or indirectly.
3. **Context** – the immediate social, practical and explicit circumstances or the pervasive influence of culture, values and implicit meanings. The first kind of context is typified by letters, telephone conversations, formal interviews, e-mail messages, a shouting match. The second includes such things as codes of politeness, shared or not shared beliefs, common experiences of life, age and gender differences, economic and social status, all unspoken but nevertheless perceived.
4. **Topic** – the topic with which this particular book is concerned is power, social and personal. The skill you will develop throughout the book is a core skill for A-Level English Language, and that is the ability to make

connections between the big, general aspects of language use, namely purpose, audience, context and topic and the little details of language actually used in a particular text, especially lexical choice and grammar.

The first three aspects are ever present when you are 'doing linguistics', whether it be stylistics, language acquisition, language varieties or language change. All the books in this series have to take each one of them into serious consideration, whatever the topic, and if you stray too far away from them in an examination answer, whatever the question, you will lose marks.

ACTIVITY 1

School Inspection

To get started, look at the following excerpt from *Kids Are Consumers Too*. It consists of guidance to teachers of American pupils aged ten and upwards on how pupils can inspect and assess the quality of provision in their school. In Britain, such inspection is routinely carried out by OfSTED inspectors.

1 Look at the language and overall style of the text, noting how it addresses the reader.

2 Next, consider some contextual factors:

a What ideas of authority and power lie behind this text?

b Is it a 'conventional' approach to English? If not, why not?

c Define the purpose and audience of this text and then identify the purpose of the children's 'Progress Report'. Is it clear just who the report is being written for? Why do you think the term 'Progress Report' has been used?

TEXT 1

Progress Report: A Straight-*A* School

Students investigate school events and/or the use of space at school. They identify areas of strength and weakness and follow a series of problem-solving tasks to bring about improvement.

Your students will earn high marks for improvements as they work together to build on strengths and promote a straight-A school!

PREPARATION Meet with the school principal and discuss the project in advance. Emphasise that the focus will be on solving problems and that he or she will be kept informed at every stage of the project. Find out whether there are any problems that students could help solve.

DISCUSSION: If you were going to make out a report card for your school, which areas would get *A*'s? (playground facilities, cafeteria, music program, parent group, and so on) Why? Which areas would get lower grades? In this project, we will work on improving these areas. When there is a problem in our city or state, how do people go about making changes? (writing to legislators, forming committees, volunteering help, voting in new laws, and so on). During your years in school, what changes or improvements have you noticed?

DIRECTIONS: Introducing the Project:

1. Let's make a list of different areas around school and events that happen (or that you'd like to see happen) at school. I'll list them on the board as you name them (areas: office, hallways, rest-rooms, cafeteria, classrooms, playground, bus stop; events: Open House, assemblies, parent conferences, class parties, Grandparents' Day, talent show, and so on).
2. (Divide students into small groups.) Within your group, select

an area or event from the list on the board that you would like to focus on. Each group should choose a different area or event. (You might want to distribute Task Card 1 to help students better understand what will be involved.)

3. (Assign groups to areas or events based on their preferences.) Each group is responsible for developing an improvement plan. You'll use a set of task cards (1) Identify a Problem, (2) List Possible Solutions, (3) Select the Best Solution, (4) Test Your Solution, and (5) Make a Progress Report. Please record your findings carefully.

Power

The Better English Campaign, in 1995, called its publicity booklet, *Language is Power*. The idea is not a new one; in the 1940s and 1950s, *Readers' Digest* was famous for its long-running monthly series entitled *Increase Your Word Power*. There is no doubt that language can have powerful effects. Shakespeare, Pope, Coleridge and Dickens were all very aware of the power of language:

For I have neither wit, nor words, nor worth
Action, nor utterance, nor power of speech,
To stir men's blood ...

from *Julius Caesar*, by William Shakespeare

Grac'd as thou art with all the Pow'r of Words,
So known, so honour'd at the House of Lords

from Epistle VI

I have strange power of speech ...

from *The Rime of the Ancient Mariner* by S T Coleridge

Language is not powerful enough to describe the infant phenomenon.

from *Nicholas Nickleby* by Charles Dickens.

Clearly, language is a great power in our lives. Works of literature, popular fiction, politics, religion and even everyday arguments, passions and comedies demonstrate this. This book, however, is not concerned so much with the power of language, as with the ways in which other forms of power in our lives use the power of language to affect the ways in which we think and behave. The persuasive elements in the language of advertising, politics and tabloid journalism are familiar enough and you will no doubt have studied some of these. There are however other, less discernible, aspects of language used by powerful social groups that have even greater effects on our minds. The topic then, is not so much 'Language and Power', as 'Power and Language'.

Speech acts

It is also important to bear in mind that language is in itself a powerful action. Certainly it is a means whereby humans think about the world they live in and communicate those thoughts to others, but it is an action as well. It is used to achieve purposes of all kinds, for example, self satisfaction, making promises, deceiving, making people laugh, swearing. Despite the age old contrast between deeds and words, there are many occasions in life when language makes things happen: solemnising a marriage, baptising, swearing an oath and other due processes of law in court proceedings. The Latin word 'rite', for example, as in 'marriage rite' and 'funeral rite' is usually thought to refer to the whole ceremony, probably because of its similarity to the word 'ritual'. It does in fact refer specifically to the words used, for it is in the power and authority vested in the speaking of those words by the person that makes a marriage, for example, or a judge's sentencing, binding.

Language in these instances may be said to have an instrumental power that not only signifies what is happening, but is the means whereby the action is accomplished: I now pronounce you man and wife . . .; The sentence of this court is . . .; I promise to pay on demand . . .; I do solemnly swear. . . . It is not difficult to see why such uses of language are referred to as 'speech acts'.

Lexis and semantics

Before exploring some examples of power in action through language, it will help to do some sorting out of your own ideas of power. The following activities are exercises in lexis and semantics, two core areas of any A-Level Language syllabus.

ACTIVITY 2

Wordpower

Take a large sheet of paper and write the word 'power' in the middle. Then think of all the words, ideas, images associated with power that come to mind, and write them down. This activity is not unlike brainstorming. Where you can see connections between words, draw lines. You may find it helpful to think of contrasting words, ideas and images and place them on opposite sides. In the 1960s, for example, flowerpower was often contrasted with firepower. You could contrast psychological power with physical power; teacher power with student power. It is likely that an intricate web will begin to grow on your sheet of paper, that will become more complex as you go on. Identify examples of power exerted by others on your life and power you exert over other people.

Work in pairs if you prefer, and finally compare your web with one or two other students.

ACTIVITY 3

Defining meaning

In the last activity you explored the lexis of power, ranging quite widely. In this activity you are going to focus more closely on semantics, that is, defining more precisely meanings of the word 'power'.

Write a definition or two of the word 'power' and compare them with the definitions below from the *Heinemann English Dictionary* (1979), a popular, pocket size school dictionary. **Don't look at the dictionary definitions first.**

power (noun)

1) the ability to act or do: a) 'most birds have the power of flight'; b) 'I'll do all in my power to help'.

2) great forcc, might or superiority: 'he seeks political power'.

3) energy available for doing work, such as that supplied by machinery as distinct from humans or animals.

power (verb)

to provide with the means of operation or activity: 'the machines are all powered by electricity'.

powerful (adjective)

having, producing or exerting power: a) 'a powerful man'; b) 'a powerful drink'.

How do your definitions compare?

Certainly, as with your own definition, there is a narrowing down of the focus. The word web you drew represents to some extent the network of interconnected ideas in your mind; the definitions are attempting to express the essence of the ideas. Notice that the words 'force', 'might', 'superiority' and 'energy' have been used in the Heinemann dictionary. What words did you use? Remember that between synonyms there is always a nuauce of different meaning.

Lexicography

You are now beginning to get involved in lexicography, a traditional and very good way of sorting out your ideas in order to find out what you really mean.

In 1981, Longman published a *Lexicon of Contemporary English.* Its compiler, Tom McArthur, explains the lexicon as follows:

'Lexicography has traditionally used the alphabet as its principal means of organising information about words. Indeed, most of us think about wordbooks as 'dictionaries', and 'dictionaries' as, necessarily, having an alphabetical order.

There has, however, been an alternative tradition, in which compilers have used other groups of topics instead of the alphabet as their basis for organisation. The alphabet, with all its virtues, places 'animals' and 'zoos', 'aunts' and 'uncles' far apart in its scheme of things, whereas in the human mind such words lie close together. The alphabetical dictionary has a logic, but it is not the logic of everyday life. In principle, one feels, words should be defined in the company they usually keep.'

ACTIVITY 4

Using a Lexicon

Look at the following entry in the *Lexicon of Contemporary English* and note any words that add ideas you may not have thought of.

Which words apply particularly to the power or importance of particular social groups and organisations?

TEXT 2

N233 *adjectives*: **strong and powerful** [B]

strong [Wa1] **1** having (a degree of) power, esp of the body: *She is not very strong after her illness. How strong is he?* **2** powerful against harm; not easily broken, spoilt, moved or changed: *He wore strong shoes. She has strong beliefs. He held the door back with his strong arm. The support of the minister puts him in a strong position in the election.* **3** [E] of a certain number: *Our club is a hundred strong* (= has 100 people in it). **4** violent: *There was a strong wind last night.* **5** powerful or effective: *His was a strong argument. There is a strong smell of cats.* **6** unacceptable: *It's a bit strong to punish them for such a small thing.* **7** (esp of drinks) having a lot of the material which gives taste: *The tea is too strong. Mix my drink strong* (= not with much water). **-ly** [adv]

intense strong (in quality or feeling): *The cold was intense. She felt intense sorrow at/over what had happened.* **-ly** [adv]

dynamic *often apprec* (of people, ideas, etc) full of or producing power and activity: *She is a very dynamic worker. His dynamic ideas helped all of us.* **-ally** [adv; Wa4]

potent **1** (of medicines, drugs, drinks, etc) having a strong and/or rapid effect on the body or mind: *This wine is too potent for me; it makes me feel unsteady.* **2** *fml* (of arguments, reasoning, etc) strongly effective; causing one to agree **3** (of a male) sexually active **4** *lit or fml* having great power, esp politically **-ly** [adv]

powerful **1** very strong; full of force: *he is a very powerful swimmer; he has powerful arms and legs. The horse had a powerful kick. It was a powerful army.* **2** of great ability; easily producing ideas: *The great scientist had a powerful brain. Her imagination is too powerful.* **3** strong or great in degree: *Onions have a powerful smell. Electric current is often powerful enough to kill. He wears powerful glasses.* **4** having a strong effect: *The minister made a powerful political speech. This wine is very powerful.* **5** having much control and influence: *Powerful nations sometimes try to frighten weaker ones.* **6** having or using great working or electrical power: *It is a powerful car with a powerful engine,* **-ly** [adv] **-ness** [U]

mighty [Wa1] *esp old use & lit* powerful; strong: *He was a mighty man and could lift whole trees.* **-tily** [adv] **-tiness** [U]

arbitrary **1** of power that is uncontrolled and used without considering the wishes of others: *The arbitrary decisions of the factory owners caused anger among the workers.* **2** *often deprec* decided by or based on personal opinion or chance rather than reason: *I didn't know anything about any of the books so my choice was quite arbitrary. Arbitrary statements have little value.* **-trarily** [adv] **-trariness** [U]

N236 *adjectives*: **not strong and powerful** [B]

weak [Wa1] **1** not strong enough to work or last properly **a** (of parts of objects): *A weak wall like that can't hold up this house.* **b** (of organs of the body): *He has a weak heart.* **2** not strong in character: *He is too weak to defend his rights.* **3** not as well as usual in body esp after illness: *His legs felt weak. My head was weak after drinking the wine.* **4** containing mainly water: *I don't like weak tea.* **5** not reaching a good standard: *His work is rather weak.* **-ly** [adv] **-ness** [U]

fragile **1** easily broken or damaged: *This old glass dish is very fragile; it's in a very fragile condition.* **2** easily destroyed; not likely to last: *Their happiness was very fragile.* **3** **a** slight in body or weak in health: *The old lady looks very fragile.* **b** *usu humor* not in a good condition of health and spirits; weak: *'I'm feeling rather fragile this morning', he said; 'I must have drunk too much (alcohol) last night'.* **fragility** [U] the condtion of being fragile

frail [Wa1] weak, esp because old and/or ill: *His health is frail. Her arms looked very frail and she couldn't lift the box.* **-ty** [U] **frailty** [U] the conditions of being frail.

feeble [Wa 1, 3] **1** very weak: *His body grew feebler as the illness got worse.* **2** very unsatisfactory: *What a feeble story; do you expect me to believe it?* **-bly** [adv] [**-ness** [U]

puny [Wa1] *usu deprec* small and weak; poorly developed: *She was a puny child, with puny little arms and legs, the result of lack of proper food. Puny man looks out at the universe.*

rickety weak in the joints and likely to break: *He was pushing a rickety old cart.*

impotent **1** having no power: *'Your army is impotent against mine!' he laughed.* **2** [Wa5] (of a male) sexually inactive **-ly** [adv]: *They watched impotently while he took the money.*

ACTIVITY 5

Using a Thesaurus

Look also at the following entries in *Roget's Thesaurus of English Words and Phrases.* First published in 1852, the Thesaurus is periodically updated to include new synonyms and antonyms. The book maps out contrasting ideas and oppositions in the ways people think. Look at the following entries and compare them with those in the Lexicon (Text 2). Add any that you find interesting to your personal mental thesaurus (your word web or ideas network). What is gained, for example, by the inclusion of words like 'authority' and 'ability'? What have they to do with power?

TEXT 3

160 Power

N. *power*, potency, mightiness 32 *greatness*; prepotency, prevalence, predominance 34 *superiority;* omnipotence, almightiness.

733 *authority*; control, sway 733 *governance*; moral power, ascendancy 178 *influence*; spiritual power, charisma, mana; witchcraft 983 *sorcery*; staying power, endurance 153 *stability*; driving force 612 *motive*; physical power, might, muscle, right arm, right hand 162 *strength*; dint, might and main, effort, endeavour 682 *exertion*; force 740 *compulsion*; stress, strain, shear; weight 322 *gravity*; weight of numbers 104 *greater number*; manpower 686 *personnel*; position of power, vantage ground 34 *advantage*; validity 494 *truth*; cogency, emphasis 532 *affirmation*; extra power, overdrive.

ability, ableness, capability, potentiality, virtuality 469 *possibility*; competence, efficiency, efficacy, effectuality 694 *skill*; capacity, faculty, virtue, property 5 *intrinsicality*; qualification 24 *fitness*; attribute 89 *concomitant*; endowment, gift 694 *aptitude*; compass, reach, grasp 183 *range*; susceptibility, affectibility 180 *liability*; trend 179 *tendency*; empowering, enablement authorization 756 *permission*.

energy, liveliness, vigour, drive, dynamism 174 *vigorousness*; internal energy, thermal e., chemical e., potential e.; work, binding energy, kinetic e., mass *or* rest e., radiant e., electrical e., atomic e., nuclear e.; mechanical energy, pedal power, engine power, horsepower; inertia, vis inertiae.

161 Impotence

N. *impotence*, lack of power, no authority, power vacuum; invalidity, impuissance 163 *weakness*; inability, incapacity; incapability, incompetence, inefficiency 728 *failure*, 695 *unskilfulness;* ineptitude, unfitness 25 *inaptitude;* decrepitude 131 *age*; frailness 114 *transience*; invalidation, disqualification 752 *abrogation*; sterility, sterilisation 172 *unproductiveness, contraception*; disarmament, demilitarisation 719 *pacification*; demobilization 75 *dispersion*.

helplessness, defencelessness 661 *vulnerability*; harmlessness 935 *innocence*; powerlessness 745 *subjection*, 747 *restraint*; impotent fury, gnashing of teeth 891 *anger*; prostration, exhaustion, inanition 684 *fatigue*; collapse, breakdown 728 *failure*; unconsciousness, faint, swoon, coma; numbness, narcosis 375 *insensibility*; stroke, apoplexy, paralysis, hemiplegia, paraplegia 651 *disease*; torpor 677 *inaction*; atrophy 655 *deterio-*

ration; senility, old age 131 *age*; ataxia, locomotor a.; loss of control, incontinence; mental decay, softening of the brain 503 *insanity*; mental weakness, imbecility 499 *unintelligence*; mutism, deaf mutism 578 *voicelessness*; legal incapacity, pupillage, minority 130 *nonage*; babyhood, infancy 130 *youth*; invalid 651 *sick person*, 163 *weakling*.

eunuch, castrato; gelding, capon, bullock, steer, neuter; freemartin, hermaphrodite.

ineffectuality, ineffectiveness, futility 497 *absurdity*; vanity 4 *insubstantiality*; uselessness 641 *inutility*; flash in the pan 114 *transcience*; dead letter, scrap of paper 752 *abrogation*; figurehead, dummy, man of straw, broken reed 4 *insubstatial thing*; empty threats, bluster 515 *empty talk*.

Adj. *powerless*, impotent, not able, unable; not enabled, unempowered, unauthorised, without authority; nominal, figurehead, constitutional 4 *insubstantial*; nugatory, invalid, null and void; unconstitutional 954 *illegal*; without a leg to stand on 163 *weak*; inoperative, not working, unexercised, unemployed 677 *nonactive*; suspended, in abeyance, cancelled, withdrawn 752 *abrogated*; abolished, swept away, gone by the board 165 *destroyed*; obsolete, on the shelf 674 *disused*; laid up, out of circulation, kaput; disqualified, deposed; unqualified, unfit, unfitted, inept 25 *unapt*; unworkable, dud, good for nothing 641 *useless*; inadequate 636 *insufficient*; ineffective, inefficacious, ineffectual, feeble 728 *unsuccessful*; incapable, incompetent, inefficient 695 *unskilful*; mechanically powerless, unpowered, unengined; unequipped 670 *unprepared*.

defenceless, helpless, without resource; bereaved, bereft 772 *losing*; kithless, kinless, orphan, unfriended 883 *friendless*; weak, harmless 935 innocent; weaponless, unarmed, disarmed 670 unequipped; unfortified, exposed, indefensible, untenable, pregnable 661 *vulnerable*.

COMMENTARY

So far you have explored ideas of power, as expressed in the words used to talk about it. You will also have thought of them in relation to different kinds of power operating in your own life.

Having explored some of the available lexis for thinking and talking about power in fairly general, abstract ways, look now at some specific examples of language data in which power of different kinds is demonstrated. All the texts have been drawn from A-Level Language examination papers in either Stylistics, Language Issues or Investigating Language Data. In every case, an ability to observe and discuss ways in which power is expressed in language would have earned marks.

ACTIVITY 6

'If you are in police detention . . .'

Below are two texts for you to compare. The context, being under police arrest, is one in which power is only too evident. The law requires the police to inform arrested persons of the powers invested in the police and of the rights to which an arrested person is entitled. Text 4 is an early draft by the police who then consulted with the Campaign for Plain English, a pressure group which aims to clarify the language of official documents. Text 5 is a revised version of the first draft.

1 Read the first text, imagining, if you like, that you have just been arrested! Make notes on your reactions as you read the document. Identify specific words and phrases that puzzle or worry you.
2 Now read the second text, noting what seem to you significant changes. What seems to be the point of the changes? Does improvement in communication lessen in any way the powers expressed in the document?

TEXT 4

DELAY OF RIGHTS

If you are in police detention suspected of having committed a serious arrestable offence and have not been charged, the rights at paragraphs 1 and 2 (over) may be conditonally delayed for up to 36 hours, if authorised by a police officer of the rank of superintendent or above.

FACILITIES PURSUANT TO PRISONERS' RIGHTS

1. If you are in police detention and your rights at paragraphs 1 and 2 (over) are not subject to delay you must be afforded the following facilities:
   a. If the person you want to be informed of your whereabouts cannot be contacted, you may choose up to two alternatives to be so informed.
   b. You may receive visits from friends or relatives at the discretion of the custody officer.
   c. You will be supplied, on request, with writing materials, your letters will be sent and you will be allowed to make one telephone call. Whether or not letters or telephone calls are at public expense shall be at the disrection of the custody officer.

2. Irrespective of whether your rights at paragraphs 1 and 2 (over) have been delayed or not, if you are a citizen of an independent Commonwealth country or a national of a foreign country you may communicate, at any time, with your High Commission, Embassy or Consulate.

FACILITIES FOR LEGAL ADVICE

If you are in police detention and your rights at paragraphs 1 and 2 (over) have not been delayed you may at any time consult and communicate privately, whether in person, in writing or on the telephone:

a. With a solicitor of your own choice
b. With the duty solicitor (where a Duty Solicitor Scheme is in operation).
c. With a solicitor selected by you from a list of solicitors who have indicated that they are available for the purpose of providing legal advice at police stations.

Please note:

Option b. above is always free.
Options a. and c. are free unless you agree otherwise with the solicitor.

FINGERPRINTS

As a general rule, your fingerprints may not be taken by the police without your consent and such consent must be in writing if you are at a police station.
Your fingerprints may be taken by the police, without consent, in the following circumstances:

a. If you are in police detention and
   i an officer of at least the rank of superintendent authorises them to be taken, such an officer having reasonable grounds for suspecting your involvement in a criminal offence and that he believes the fingerprints will tend to confirm or disprove your involvement in the offence; or
   ii you have been charged with a recordable offence and have not had your fingerprints taken in the course of the investigation of the offence.
b. If you have been convicted of a recordable offence.

TEXT 5

Your four rights

1 The right to have someone told where you are.

2 The right to seek legal advice.

3 The right to read the Codes of Practice made under the Police and Criminal Evidence Act, 1984.

4 The right to receive, on request, a copy of your custody record on release. This right lasts for 12 months after release.

Can the police delay my rights?

It is lawful for an officer of at least the rank of superintendent to delay Rights 1 and 2 for up to 36 hours if:

- you are suspected of a serious arrestable offence*, *and*
- you have not been charged.

But the officer must *also* have good reason to believe that to allow Rights 1 and 2 would:

- interfere with evidence or interfere with or harm another person, *or*
- lead to the alerting of other people suspected of an offence, *or*
- hinder the recovery of property obtained by crime.

If you are a citizen of an independent Commonwealth country or you are a national of a foreign country you always have the right to communicate with your High Commission, Embassy or Consulate. This right cannot be delayed or stopped.

What must the police allow me to do?

(*This section only applies if Rights 1 and 2 have not been delayed*)

- Right 1 says you may ask for someone to be told where you are. If this person cannot be contacted, you may choose up to two other people to be told.
- You may receive visits from friends or relatives if the custody officer agrees.
- If you ask for writing materials you will be given them. Your letters will be sent and you will be allowed to make one phone call. The custody officer will decide whether you will have to pay for postage and phone calls.

How can I get legal advice?

The custody officer will give you a leaflet which explains:

- how to get legal advice,
- whether it will be free or not.

When may the police take my fingerprints?

Normally the police may not take your fingerprints without your agreement. And if you are at a police station your agreement must be in writing.
However, the police may take your fingerprints without your agreement if you are in police detention and *either*:

- an officer of at least the rank of superintendent says they may be taken. Such an officer must have good reason for suspecting you are involved in a criminal offence and that he believes the fingerprints may confirm or disprove it, *or*
- you have been charged with a recordable offence* and have not had your fingerprints taken during the investigation of the offence.

The police may also take your fingerprints without your agreement if you have been convicted of a recordable offence.

**Please ask the custody officer if you are not sure what these terms mean.*

The information on this side of the form is only a summary of the law to help you understand your rights. It is not a full statement of the law.

COMMENTARY

None of the comments below invalidate your own observations. They illustrate a linguistic approach to the texts and should be included with your own.

- Notice the use of the second person pronoun ('you' and 'your') throughout Text 4 which makes the text entirely confrontational. In Text 5 not only are questions introduced, but there is also the use of the first person ('I, me, my') which offsets the directive use of the second person.
- Whereas the opening sentences of Text 4 contain four conditionals (ie statements/declaratives beginning with 'if'), Text 5 begins with a list of rights. In other words, Text 4 states conditions including the unexplained term 'conditionally delayed', while Text 5 establishes immediately what the arrested person's rights are.
- There is a further recognition in Text 5 that the term 'recordable offence' may not be understood. It is interesting though, that because it is a specific legal term it has to be retained and cannot be paraphrased, hence the asterisked note (*Please ask…)
- Notice that in both documents there are important anaphoric references (ie references to earlier parts). In Text 4, however, the references to Rights 1 and 2 are inconveniently over the page, whereas Text 5 incorporates them on the same page.
- The purpose of the text is to inform an audience that is literally a captive one. Information is often a form of power; keeping it secret creates unjust power; making information freely available shares the power. In this instance the authority and power to arrest a citizen carries with it the responsibility to maintain all the other democratic laws that govern both the police and those under arrest. Note that the Plain English Campaign has added a final note informing readers that the text 'is not a full statement of the law'.

Language and Social Context

In an interview for *e-magazine* (August 1998), Basil Bernstein observed that a significant contribution made by Norman Fairclough to linguistics is his insistence that to abstract language from its social contexts is to take away much of its meaning. Nowhere is this better demonstrated than in the two texts discussed below.

ACTIVITY 7

What does the Charter do?

The text below consists of Sections 2, 3 and 4 of the *Kirklees Community Care Charter.* Interestingly, the cover bears a Plain English Campaign logo which states, 'Plain Language and Clear Print, Plainly Better'.

One distinctive feature of life in the 1990s has been the introduction of Charters governing a wide range of social activities: Passenger Charters, Patients' Charters, Parents' Charters, Customer Charters. Essentially they are concerned with accountability.

1. Read the text and note any features that seem significant to you. Consider closely purpose and audience and how the authors set up their frame of reference (eg definitions, terms, scope).
2. Find out if your school or college has a student charter or similar document. You may have had to sign an agreement of some kind. Compare it with the charter here.

TEXT 6

2

ਇਹ 'ਕਮਿਊਨਿਟੀ ਕੇਅਰ ਡੌਕੂਮੈਂਟ (ਸਮਾਜੀ ਦੇਖ-ਭਾਲ ਦੀ ਯੋਜਨਾ)' ਸੰਬੰਧੀ ਦਸਤਾਵੇਜ਼ ਉਰਦੂ, ਗੁਜਰਾਤੀ, ਪੰਜਾਬੀ, ਚੀਨੀ, ਅਤੇ ਪੋਲਿਸ਼ ਭਾਸ਼ਾਵਾਂ ਵਿਚ ਉਪਲੱਬਧ ਹੈ । ਇਹ ਬ੍ਰੇਲ ਅਤੇ ਔਡੀਓ ਟੇਪ (ਸੁਣਨ ਵਾਲੀ ਟੇਪ) ਤੇ ਵੀ ਮਿਲ ਸਕਦਾ ਹੈ । ਇਸ ਦੀ ਕਾਪੀ ਲੈਣ ਲਈ (01484) 225214 ਨੰਬਰ ਤੇ ਫ਼ੋਨ ਕਰੋ ।

આ 'કોમ્યુનિટી કેર પ્લાન' (સામાજની દેખભાળનું આયોજન)નો દસ્તાવેજ ઉર્દુ, ગુજરાતી, પંજાબી ચાઈનીસ અને પોલીશ ભાષાઓમાં મળી શકે છે. એ બ્રેઈલ લીપી અને ઓડિયો ટેપ પર પણ મળી શકે છે. નકલો મેળવવા માટે મહેરબાની કરી (01484) 225214 નંબર પર ટેલીફોન કરો.

یہ دستاویز - کمیونٹی کیئر پلان - (کمیونٹی کی دیکھ بھال کا منصوبہ) اردو، گجراتی، پنجابی، چینی، اور پولش زبان میں بھی مل سکتی ہے ۔ اس کے علاوہ نابینوں کی زبان - بریل - اور آڈیو ٹیپ کی شکل میں بھی دستیاب آپ کو چاہیے ہوں تو اس نمبر پر فون کریں: 01484 225214

Niniejsze założenia planu Opieki Społecznej można uzyskać w językach: Gujirati, Punjabi, chińskim i polskim. Są one też dostępne w wydaniu braila i na taśmach. Po egzemplarze proszę zgłaszać się pod numer telefonu: 01484 225214.

此份社區護理計劃文件有烏爾都文、古扎華提文、旁遮普文、中文與波蘭文譯本，亦有凸字與錄音帶版本，請電01484 225 214索取一份。

This document is available in Gujerati, Urdu, Punjabi, Polish and Chinese. It is also available in Braille and on audio tape. For copies, please telephone (01484) 225214.

ਕਮਿਊਨਿਟੀ ਕੇਅਰ, ਤੁਹਾਨੂੰ ਤੁਹਾਡੇ ਚੁਣੇ ਹੋਏ ਤਰੀਕੇ ਨਾਲ ਜ਼ਿੰਦਗੀ ਗੁਜ਼ਾਰਨ ਲਈ ਮਦਦ ਦੇਣ ਵਾਸਤੇ ਹੈ। ਜਿੰਨਾਂ ਮੁਮਕਿਨ ਹੋਵੇ, ਵੱਧ ਤੋਂ ਵੱਧ ਸਮੇਂ ਲਈ, ਤੁਹਾਨੂੰ ਤੁਹਾਡੇ ਘਰ ਵਿਚ ਹੀ ਰਹਿਣ ਲਈ ਮਦਦ ਮਿਲੇ ਜਾਂ ਸਮਾਜ ਵਿਚ ਘਰੇਲੂ ਮਾਹੌਲ ਵਿਚ ਰਹਿਣ ਲਈ ਮਦਦ ਮਿਲੇ। ਤੁਹਾਨੂੰ ਤੁਹਾਡੀ ਉਮਰ, ਅਪਾਹਜਤਾ ਜਾਂ ਦਿਮਾਗੀ ਬਿਮਾਰੀ ਦੀ ਵਜ੍ਹਾ ਕਰਕੇ ਸ਼ਾਇਦ ਮਦਦ ਦੀ ਲੋੜ ਹੋਵੇ।

કોમ્યુનિટી કેર આપની પસંદ કરેલી જીવન પદ્ધતિ પ્રમાણે રહેવામાં આપને સહકાર આપવા વિષે છે. એનો અર્થ એ કે આપને કયાં તો આપના પોતાના ઘરમાં રહેવામાં અથવા તો જ્યાં સુધી વાજબી રીતે શક્ય હોય ત્યાં સુધી સમાજમાં ઘર જેવા વાતાવરણમાં રાખવામાં સહકાર આપવો. ઉંમર, અપંગતા અથવા માનસિક બિમારીને કારણે આ કરવા માટે કદાચ આપને મદદની જરૂર પડશે.

کمیونٹی کیئر کا تعلق آپ کو اپنی مرضی کی زندگی گزارنے میں مدد دینے سے ہے ۔ اس کا مطلب یہ ہے کہ جب تک ممکن ہو آپ کو اپنے گھر میں یا کمیونٹی کے اندر گھر جیسے ماحول میں رہنے میں مدد و حمایت فراہم کی جائے ۔ آپ کو مختلف وجوہات کی بناء پر اس مدد کی ضرورت پڑ سکتی ہے ۔ جیسے بڑھاپا ، معذوری یا ذہنی بیماری ۔

Praca usług społecznych polega na zapewnianiu Wam trybu życia przez Was wybranego. To znaczy, umożliwieniu Wam mieszkania we własnym domu, lub domowym otoczeniu w Waszym środowisku społecznym tak długo, jak to będzie możliwe. Możecie dlatego wymagać pomocy ze względu na Wasz wiek, inwalidztwo lub chorobę psychiczną.

社區護理的用意是支持你以你所選擇的生活方式生活，這即是說支持你留在家中，或是在社區內如家般的環境中，盡可能合理地生活得多久就多久。你可能因為年紀、傷殘或精神病而需要幫忙去這樣做。

Community care is about supporting you to live your chosen way of life. It means supporting you to stay either in your home, or in a homely environment in the community, for as long as reasonably possible. You might need help to do this because of age, disability or mental illness.

97/98

5

Community care services are provided for children as well as for adults. More details on services and plans for children and young people can be found in the Children's Plan **Young Citizens**.

Who provides community care services?

Most community care is provided by relatives, friends and neighbours. Help is also provided by social services, the health services and housing services. The private sector and voluntary organisations also provide services. Many other services linked to community care are provided by the council such as transport, leisure facilities, libraries and adult education.

If you want to know more about services, see the Community Care Guide.

3. What does the Charter do?

The charter is for users and carers. It:

- sets out standards for what you can expect from social services, health services and housing services.
- gives you some specific standards for particular services
- tells you who to contact if things go wrong

The charter is also for staff who provide community care services. It explains what is expected of them and what they should be aiming to achieve.

97/98

6

4. Shared standards

These are general standards that social services, health services and housing services have a commitment to.

You can expect:

- to be treated with courtesy
- to be treated in a way that does not discriminate against you
- to have any needs arising from language, cultural beliefs, religion or disability taken into account
- to know the name and job title of the person you are dealing with
- to be involved in discussions about your care and have your preferences taken into account
- to be kept informed when decisions are made about you and about changes
- as a carer, to have your needs taken into account
- to receive a written care plan
- to have your care plan regularly reviewed
- to be registered with a GP and, if needed, to get help to register
- to have access to your records which are kept by housing services, social services and health services
- to know that these personal records will be confidential and only shared with other agencies if you consent or where it is necessary to provide a service

97/98

COMMENTARY

- Notice the Charter's multilingual introduction. Making information available in a person's first language is a particularly empowering action. The whole Charter is in fact available in different languages.
- As in the police document, it is important to define exactly what is what (what is community care?) and who is who (who are 'users' and 'carers'?).
- Notice the term 'shared standards' which implies cooperation. 'Shared' is certainly a persuasive, reassuring word, while 'standards', a word of the 1990s, implies something that both parties of the Charter can recognise independently. In other words the power exercised by the 'carers' is not arbitrary.
- As in the revised police document, the illusion of a dialogue is created by the use of a question and answer format. This, however, is a double-edged strategy, for while it looks like the reader is participating in the text it also usurps or deflects an important power possessed by all readers, namely the power to ask their own questions. You may feel this is a small price to pay in the overall intention of the writers (carers) to put themselves in the place of the readers (users).

ACTIVITY 8

Students are ignored ...

The text below was written for students to inform them of their liability/exemption in the payment of Council Tax.

1. Read the text, noting words or phrases that strike you as particularly significant.
2. Pay particular attention to the last section. Can you understand it?

TEXT 7

WHO IS A STUDENT?

Under the new Council Tax legislation, you may qualify as a student if you are: an adult following a full-time course or qualifying course of education, a foreign language assistant, or a student nurse on a Project 2000 course.
To qualify as a student you must:

EITHER

(a) be a person taking a full-time course of education, which lasts for at least one academic/calendar year.

- attend for 24 weeks of the year.
- attend for at least 21 hours of each week for study, tuition or work experience.
- attend a prescribed educational estabishment, e.g. university or college.

OR

(b) be taking a qualifying course of education, such as B Tec, 'A' levels.

- be under 20 years of age.
- be taking a course which lasts for at least 3 calendar months.
- be taking a further education course and not higher education course.
- attend the course for more than 12 hours each week.
- not be taking a correspondence course.

- not be on day release.
- normally attend the course between 8.00a.m. and 5.30pm.

Foreign Language Assistant

To qualify as a foreign language assistant you must:

- be registered with the Central Bureau for Educational Visits and Exchanges

  AND

- be appointed as a foreign language assistant at a school or other education establishment in Great Britain.

Student Nurses

To qualify as a Student Nurse you must be following one of these courses:

- Project 2000
- Student Midwives
- Student Health Visitors

  AND

- you must be studying to qualify for the first time for inclusion on the United Kingdom Central Council for Nursing, Midwifery and Health Visiting (UKCC) Register.

WHAT DO STUDENTS PAY?

This will depend on whether you are the Council Tax payer and the circumstances of the household.

Under Community Charge full-time students were expected to pay 20% of the charge, this is no longer the case with Council Tax.

In general, students defined as above will be '**exempt**' and will not pay the Council Tax if they live in Halls of Residence, or a property occupied wholly by students.

However, Council Tax will be payable where a household only partly consists of students. Students are ignored (**disregarded**) when counting the number of adults in a property (*see information Leaflet No. 3*).

After those people who are ignored (disregarded) have been taken into account, if there are two or more people left in the property the full Council Tax will be payable.

COMMENTARY

Notice again, the need to establish who is who and what is what. Terms of reference are a prime consideration. The purpose of this text is to inform students, not likely to be earners or property owners, of exemptions and liabilities. It describes a policy that is intended to be ethical.

- Notice the importance of the word 'qualify' – a power word if ever there was one!
- Notice also the grammatical structure, 'you may ... if ...' at the beginning, followed by a sequence of four 'musts'. 'May' is used here in the sense of possibility. It is a modal verb, modifying 'qualify'. The word

'must' however, is a deontic modal, which means to say it expresses power by insisting on compliance with specifications. There are no two ways about it!

- The choice of words at the end is surprising. 'Ignored' seems oddly unsuitable in its everyday sense yet seems to have a technical sense which the local authority is required to observe. The gloss provided, 'disregard', is clearly regarded as less likely to cause misunderstanding.

ACTIVITY 9

That's a good idea

The following text is a transcript taken from Deborah Tannen's *Talking From 9 to 5* (1994), a study of the different ways in which men and women talk to each other at work.

A manager, Sid, is discussing with his secretary, Rita, preparations for an impending visit by several high level managers from a regional office.

Read the transcript, an excerpt from a longer conversation, and describe the style of the conversation. Is, for example, Rita's role entirely subordinate? Note down any feature of language that reflects the influence of context.

TEXT 8

Sid: Oh and I was meaning to ask you about that. When I meet them Sunday, I'll have the invi-invitation for Sunday night's activities, and also I'll have an agenda, for the following day? In fact an agenda for the following week, for them – to give them, is that right?

Rita: Well, we can – we can do that.

Sid: So that – so that that night they can plan on, they can just look down through the agenda and see where they're going the next day, and we don't just present it to them Monday morning first thing.

Rita: That's a very good idea. I'll uh –

Sid: And, uh, if it could just be in an envelope or something for each of them and when I give them the invitation I can give them also the agenda showing them what the – what is going to happen for not only Monday but Tuesday and Wednesday, they've got the whole three days laid out.

Rita: That's a very good idea. Okay we'll see if we can have a whole lot of things for you to present to them.

Sid: Okay. All right, yep, that's a good idea.

COMMENTARY

- From the context and status of the participants it is reasonable to assume that managers exercise more power of decision than secretaries. (Note here that a mental network of power meanings needs to include such distinctions as 'power to make decisions' as opposed to, say, 'financial power' or 'brute force'.)
- Certainly Sid says more than Rita and his questions at the beginning are in fact instructions. We can assume a rising tone to 'I'll have the invi-invitation . . .'. Notice that the polite form 'ask' really means 'tell'. Notice also, Rita's slight hesitation as she interprets correctly that she is being instructed. Sid goes on to explain why a prepared agenda would be helpful and is reassured by Rita. He then goes on to give Rita instructions in an indirect way using an 'if . . .' structure. Rita reassures him again and promises, albeit guardedly, to have 'a whole lot of things'

ready. Sid's final remark confirms his reassurance four times: 'Okay. All right, yep, that's a good idea.'

- Sid exercises power as an initiator and as the person ultimately responsible for the success of the plan – he's the boss. But he is not directly bossy, and Rita too exercises power as a reassuring influence, since Sid seeks reassurance and is effectively reassured in the end.

When this passage was set in an examination, a number of candidates saw Sid as a power monster and Rita as not only a power slave but a gender victim as well. It is true that Sid does most of the talking and that he even interrupts Rita at one point. Undoubtedly there is an historically and culturally accumulated gender bias evident in modern offices and reflected here, but the linguistic evidence in this particular conversation points to cooperativeness and shared control of the conversation. It typifies the kind of 'thinking aloud' planning that needs a listener on the same wavelength and able to participate.

What also needs to be taken into account is the influence of organisational culture. There are unspoken codes at work here influencing how office conversations (or discourse) should be conducted. Personal style and manner (idiolect) have to be modified to fit the office style (a kind of business dialect, or sociolect, if you prefer to restrict the word dialect to regional variations). The need to learn a style of talk is yet further proof of how prevailing power of any kind will influence language uses and styles.

ACTIVITY 10

Have you been worrying about your health?

The following transcript records part of a doctor/patient interview. Read it, and note the following:

- the frequency and type of questions
- any interruptions
- the unspoken rules for such a conversation (pragmatics)

TEXT 9

Doctor: Who's in the house with you?
Patient: The wife.
Doctor: Just the two of you?
Patient: Yes.
Doctor: Have you got any brothers and sisters?
Patient: Yes.
Doctor: How many have you got?
Patient: Three brothers and one sister.
Doctor: Are they all fit and well?
Patient: Yes, uhuh.
Doctor: There's nobody with blood pressure trouble in the family?
Patient: No.
Doctor: Or kidney trouble in the family?
Patient: No.
Doctor: Do you know anybody with heart trouble?
Patient: My mother died when she was 56 with heart trouble. That was in 1960.
Doctor: Anybody else?
Patient: No.
Doctor: Nobody else in the family?
Patient: Not in our direct family.

Doctor: Sure?
Patient: Not in the immediate family.
Doctor: Are you a worrier by nature, do you think?
Patient: Yes, I think I am. I think actually I am.
Doctor: Have you had any particular worries recently, or are you
Patient Well my son's living in London and he's not got a secure job, you know. I'm not sure about him so – I know we shouldn't be worried about him, he's 24 next month, but
Doctor: How many children have you got actually?
Patient: Just the one.
Doctor: Have you been worrirying about your health?

From 'Approaches to describing doctor–patient interviews' by Joan Maclean in *Working with Language* (1989), ed by Hywel Coleman.

COMMENTARY

The doctor's questions, which look on the page like a barrage, are being asked to elicit information needed for diagnosis. Patients comply with the established format of medical consultations because they trust (have to trust) the power and authority possessed by the doctor through specialist knowledge and training. Virtually all the questions are closed, requiring yes/no or one-word answers. Note though that the patient does actually interrupt the doctor at one point when the doctor's question about worries seems to trigger off a longer response. It is clear that the doctor knows exactly where he is going. All that is expected of the patient is clear and accurate answers. Note how the doctor checks one of the answers (line 23). Note too how the doctor, at the end, steers the consultation back to the patient's health.

ACTIVITY 11

Fetch a policeman

The last text brings you back to the context of legal power, the point where this series of activities started. It is a transcript of part of a hearing in the Maintenance and Arrears section of a Magistrates' Court. Note the power implication of the word 'hearing'. Who is authorised to 'listen'? Note how the Court is placed in the receptive role and the 'defendant' in the productive. As you will see, he has to give an account of himself.

Read the transcript and make notes on the following:

- the use of questions (who asks them?)
- other types of utterance from the magistrate
- any signs of a shift in who is controlling the hearing
- the direct exercise of power and how it is enacted.

TEXT 10

Note: Numbers in brackets indicate the length of pauses in seconds.

Magistrate: do you understand
(6)
Mr A: yeh
Magistrate: you understand
Mr A: yeh
Magistrate: that's good – now you've given us your number and you've given us your firm – and the office will be in touch with – the office will be in touch with them

Mr A:	I'm going to leave there
Magistrate:	pardon
Mr A:	I'm leaving there
Magistrate:	why are you leaving there
	(4)
Mr A:	cause I don't want to pay that
Magistrate:	why not (2) Mr. A. what do you mean you don't *want* to pay – don't you realize you've got an order *to* pay
Mr A:	yeh – well if I'd have wanted to pay I'd have paid before wouldn't I
Magistrate:	I don't know – at all
Mr A:	yeh
Magistrate:	there's lots of reasons why people don't pay
Mr A:	I just don't want to – I'll pay to me children – yes – but not to *her*
Magistrate:	well if you flatly refuse to *accept* the order of the court there's only one alternative – then you'll go to prison
Mr A:	yeh
Magistrate:	is that what you're saying
Mr A:	yes
Magistrate:	will you fetch a policeman [to the usher]
Mr A:	you can't do it now (2) I'm still uh under psychiatric treatment
Magistrate:	you can receive that in prison Mr–uh A
Mr A:	oh thank you [with ironic intonation]
	(5)
Magistrate:	you can't tell – you can't refuse to do something and tell us what we can do at the same time you know
Mr A:	that's the system in't it

From 'The Form and Function of Threats in Court' by Sandra Harris in *Language and Communication* 4(4)

COMMENTARY

From the context you know that power and authority reside in the magistrate (look up the meaning of the alternative name, Justice of the Peace; check also the etymology of 'magistrate' to see what power meaning is encoded there). Mr A would have found himself under arrest if he had not attended the hearing and indeed faces the possibility of arrest anyway, for his resistance. Notice that the magistrate is concerned that Mr A understands what is going on. His second utterance confers approval on Mr A's answer, 'that's good', a sure sign of authority. It's an example of a conversational triple in which the normal pattern of paired exchanges (see the opening question paired with an answer) is broken by the addition of an underlining, evaluative remark. Frequently, a word such as 'good', 'okay', 'right', 'fine' is used. 'That's good' can also mean, 'We can get on with the matter in hand'. From that point on however, it becomes clear that the magistrate is not going to get the answers he would prefer. Notice, for example, the pattern of Mr A's utterances after his first 'yeh': contradiction, repeated contradiction, negative statement, rhetorical question, affirmative, negative statement, including a positive alternative, confirmation, confirmation, negative protest, ironic thankyou, rhetorical question.

If the magistrate's order to the usher to fetch a policeman is a threat, it has a powerful effect on Mr A. Note though, how the magistrate uses a polite form to the usher: 'will you fetch . . .'.

Mr A's final remark wonderfully encapsulates his awareness of impotence in the face of legal power: 'that's the system in't it'. He remains resistant to the bitter end.

Questions

Questions are a distinctive feature of both of the last two transcripts. You have also seen earlier how the question/answer format is popular in otherwise non-interactional information texts (eg the Community Care Charter). It is easy to see how questions can be an exercise of power and authority in, for example, legal interrogations, income tax returns, medical consultations, official enquiries, school inspections. Remember though that they can also question authority; they can turn a conversation in another direction and raise awkward issues. Answering a question with a question is a well known way of taking control of a conversation.

This chapter has introduced you to a major aspect of 'Language and Society', namely the exercise and expression of power by individuals and social organisations through spoken and written discourse (the texts and transcripts).

You should have begun to sort out in your own mind, various meanings of the word 'power' and begun to recognise that language study is not just a matter of looking at the words and the grammar but of appreciating also the social contexts in which language is used. It is all a matter of connecting little 'bits' of language in a text (choice of words, grammatical features) to the bigger aspects of communication through language (type of discourse, purpose of communication, social context).

In looking at the texts you have added to your stylistics repertoire an awareness of power structures that have a direct bearing on the ways in which language is used. You will have found too that a concept of 'power', to be useful, needs to be supported in its meaning by other ideas such as 'authority', 'responsibility', 'rights', 'liability', 'consent', all of which occur in, or are directly relevant to, one or other of the texts you have investigated. These things lie behind and are even woven into texts. Ron Carter, in *Seeing Through Language* (CUP, 1990), uses the double meaning of his title in the sense of scanning the text (looking through it to see what is in it), and looking through and beyond it to see the values and assumptions lying below the surface or behind the words. You have also observed strategies whereby power and control are exercised in speech and writing.

Your own role as a reader is critical here, and will become more so as you progress through the book. You will need to read very accurately at the literal level (the actual words) but also at the inferential level (the unspoken, unwritten signs in the spaces in-between). In the commentaries you will have noticed a number of references to things in the texts, even direct quotations, but they were used to point to their explanation or to their significance. If you only paraphrase or retell bits of text, you only tell your reader (the examiner!) what is already there. Stylistics of any kind must do more than that. For the purposes of this book, it must say something about power and language.

2 Discourse and Power

In this chapter you will:

- explore ideas and definitions of two keywords, 'Discourse' and 'Ideology'
- investigate the discourse and ideologies of political journalism
- revisit and develop further, ideas and definitions of power
- investigate the discourse of Girl Power.

People live not only in a world of concrete objects that they can buy, own, lose and bump into, they also live with abstract nouns (freedom, identity, love) and evaluative adjectives (good, bad, nice, nasty) which do not have any obvious 'real' existence but plenty of tangible effects in life. 'Power' is itself an abstract noun that can mean many things, but the moment you compound it with a concrete noun the meaning becomes clear:

horsepower, manpower, girlpower, powertool, powerbrakes, powerpack.

Throughout this book, abstract nouns will occur from time to time. This may not be a very exciting prospect; you may even feel a headache coming on, but these words are a part of modern linguistics and in one way or another affect everybody's life and thought. First, discourse.

Discourse

Living Language describes discourse as either the 'general ways in which people talk and write about particular subject areas' or as 'a stretch of language longer than a single utterance or sentence'. These are complementary definitions.

Two notable thinkers about language and society are Michel Foucault (*The Order of Discourse*, 1970) and Norman Fairclough (*Discourse and Social Change*, 1992). Both stress the importance of discourse not just as a sequence of words (eg a letter, a novel, an advertisement, a history lecture, a scientific paper) but as a specialised field of knowledge and distinctive language use (consider economics, religion, the book you are reading at this minute). Each field has its own meanings, terms, frames of reference, language conventions, communication styles and sets of values. The term 'orders of discourse' refers to the distinctive ways in which specific groups communicate with each other, for example, lawyers with clients, teachers with students, probation officers with probationers, media producers with their audiences, advertisers with consumers, supermarkets with customers.

Any large institution will have a characteristic discourse and will contain within itself different orders of discourse – a hospital, a college, a business, a theatre. Discourse within a family is probably the most familiar and reassuring kind, and it is not surprising that some large organisations like to promote themselves as 'one big happy family'. This is an attempt to reduce alienation, anonymity and perceived lack of communication. It could be sincere; it could be a con.

A look at popular expressions gives clues about rule-governed or convention-bound discourses within a family:

- I won't have you talking like that in this house.
- I know mealtime is not the right occasion, but . . .
- Don't talk to me like that!
- Who do you think you're talking to?
- We'll have less of that kind of talk, young lady!
- Go and ask your father.
- I couldn't talk to my parents about it.
- She needs a good talking to.

ACTIVITY 12

Family Talk

Make a list of some of the unwritten rules for who talks to whom about what, and how, in your family.

1 What sorts of topics may or may not be discussed?
2 Whose talk matters most?
3 What sorts of things are implied or left unsaid?
4 What levels of feeling are evident? Affection? Irritation?
5 What are the occasions and contexts for family talk?
6 Identify two different orders of discourse in family talk.

Discourse in Journalism

In the field of journalism there are different orders of discourse. Here are some examples:

- interviews between reporters and people in the news
- discussions between reporters and editors about slanting, angling or doctoring the spin of a story or news item
- interactions between readers and a newspaper.

The latter example is evidenced not only by the implied approval of a reader's regular buying of the paper, but also in readers' letters, another order of discourse.

ACTIVITY 13

1 Collect a selection of readers' letters (about ten). Decide whether you wish to range over a number of papers and magazines or focus on one. Investigate the following:

- opening strategies
- tone adopted (eg indignation, congratulation, anxiety)
- purpose and topic
- closing strategies
- who appears to be addressed.

Remember that letters may be edited.

2 Now look at an item in a newspaper about which you have a point of view and write to the editor. Think of the kind of discourse you are getting into and write in an appropriate style. You could, alternatively, reply to one of the letters.

Robert Hodge, in *Historical Semantics and the Meanings of Discourse* (1984) adds a further dimension to the idea of discourse. He points out the following aspects: participation, interaction and shared perceptions.

Teachers, lawyers, doctors, social workers, students, party politicians, police, terrorists, priests, advertisers, sales representatives, all make sense of the world in their own ways. This does not necessarily exclude other ways of looking at life, but it will play a dominant part in their working lives and may also affect outlook in other areas of life. Note that 'semantics' in Hodge's title means 'making sense of life'.

Individuals belong to different social groups and in each group, participate in the appropriate discourse automatically. A sociologist would say that by this participation and interaction, people are socialised into ways of thinking and behaving. You can often tell what groups people belong to by the way they talk. Within a discourse, certain things will be taken for granted, will seem like common sense. The things that are taken for granted may, of course, not seem like common sense to someone who doesn't participate in a particular kind of discourse. It will not be shared. Newspapers depend a great deal on this kind of mind reading.

Consider the following example.

The Gulf War

Look at the following text from the *Guardian* newspaper 23 January 1991.

TEXT 11

Mad dogs and Englishmen

We have	**They have**
Army, Navy and Air Force	A war machine
Reporting guidelines	Censorship
Press briefings	Propaganda
We	**They**
Take out	Destroy
Suppress	Destroy

Eliminate	Kill
Neutralise or decapitate	Kill
Decapitate	Kill
Dig in	Cower in their foxholes
We launch	**They launch**
First strikes	Sneak missile attacks
Pre-emptively	Without provocation
Our men are . . .	**Their men are . . .**
Boys	Troops
Lads	Hordes
Our boys are . . .	**Theirs are . . .**
Professional	Brainwashed
Lion-hearts	Paper tigers
Cautious	Cowardly
Confident	Desperate
Heroes	Cornered
Dare-devils	Cannon fodder
Young knights of the skies	Bastards of Baghdad
Loyal	Blindly obedient
Desert rats	Mad dogs
Resolute	Ruthless
Brave	Fanatical
Our boys are motivated by	**Their boys are motivated by**
An old fashioned sense of duty	Fear of Saddam
Our boys	**Their boys**
Fly into the jaws of hell	Cower in concrete bunkers
Our ships are . . .	**Iraq ships are . . .**
An armada	A navy
Israeli non-retaliation is	**Iraqi non-retaliation is**
An act of great statesmanship	Blundering/Cowardly
The Belgians are . . .	**The Belgians are also . . .**
Yellow	Two-faced
Our missiles are . . .	**Their missiles are . . .**
Like Luke Skywalker zapping Darth Vader	Ageing duds (*rhymes with Scuds*)
Our missiles cause . . .	**Their missiles cause . . .**
Collateral damage	Civilian casualties
We . . .	**They . . .**
Precision bomb	Fire wildly at anything in the skies
Our PoWs are . . .	**Their PoWs are . . .**
Gallant boys	Overgrown schoolchildren
George Bush is . . .	**Saddam Hussein is . . .**
At peace with himself	Demented
Resolute	Defiant
Statesmanlike	An evil tyrant
Assured	A crackpot monster
Our planes . . .	**Their planes . . .**
Suffer a high rate of attrition	Are shot out of the sky
Fail to return from missions	Are Zapped

COMMENTARY

During the Gulf War, the *Guardian* kept track of how the war was reported in other papers. The list on the left contains terms used to describe UN and US forces, while the terms on the right referred to Iraqi forces. Together they demonstrate very clearly how an 'us' and 'them' outlook is constructed. By selecting vocabulary (lexis) to describe the UN/US forces in neutral terms whilst describing the Iraqi forces in provocative and emotive terms, the social convention of loyalty to the 'home team' has been invoked. This social convention assigns a legitimate role to the UN/US forces and an illegitimate role to the Iraqi forces. In other words unequal power relations have been established in the mind. The taken-for-granted, preferred view is that UN/US forces were justified in intervening in the Gulf War. The discourse clearly encodes thoughts and attitudes that are expected to be shared.

There is a further dimension to this particular example. In 1997, Martin Bell, the former BBC foreign correspondent, made a series of TV programmes about news reporting for Radio 4, *The Truth Is Our Currency.* He spoke about the restrictions imposed by the UN/US forces on war reporters. His own reports were 'edited' and 'sanitised' away from the war zone before being broadcast from London. Thus, in addition to patriotic, emotional and moral bias in war reporting, it is also very easy to introduce inaccuracies or to exclude information that will in fact make the very things taken for granted, a distortion of what really happened.

Readers remain free to believe anything they see in print. The point here is not to argue the rights and wrongs of politics in the Middle East, but to show how discourse constructs in our minds ideas, attitudes and beliefs that may or may not reflect reality but which we have taken for granted because of the sheer power of the printed word and media bulletins.

The following examples will give you an opportunity to examine other examples of discourse and underlying assumptions.

ACTIVITY 14

The British people at war

The following passage is an introduction to a book of photographs taken by journalists in Britain and published sometime during the 1939–45 war. The book is entitled *The British People At War*. Read the passage and answer the following questions:

1 The book was published for British readers in time of war: what effect is achieved by writing about them in the third person?

2 What political views are assumed or implied?

3 What attitudes are expected of the reader?

4 How far would you call this kind of writing 'propaganda'?

5 The element of participation in a discourse means that readers have been assigned a role by the writers. What role has the reader been assigned here?

6 What social conventions are being invoked, for example, attitudes toward one's own country?

7 What is the taken-for-granted view of the world behind this text?

8 Are there any contextual factors influencing the text?

TEXT 12

The British People go to War

At 11.0 a.m. on September 3rd, 1939, Britain entered a new era. The transition from peace to war was swift and dramatic. The country had put on uniform. The sky, over the cities was dotted with balloons. Everywhere, people were digging trenches, filling sandbags. Gas masks were being given out. There was a rush for black paper and cloth to screen windows and skylights. Grim, grey vehicles thundered along the roads on mysterious errands. There was in the air a feeling of change, complete, inevitable, tremendous.

Every British household had felt war was brewing though none could anticipate exactly what it would be like. Now, in their quiet way, the people got busy. There was work to do, no time to waste in regrets for week-ends by the sea, quiet evenings at home, tennis, bridge-parties, and all the rest of the pleasant little details of their previous existence. The world might be upside down. If so, they must learn to be upside down too. They must do all sorts of things they had never done before. They must adapt themselves to conditions that had never existed before at all. They did all this with cheerfulness for they saw that it was necessary. The British might be a little weak on geography and the nicer distinctions of political theories: but they were quite clear on the difference between being free men and women and being slaves. The totalitarian powers of Europe had put the issue before them and as the free people of a democratic state they had made the choice deliberately.

The subsequent adventures of the average and representative citizen may be followed in these pages. The boys are in the Army, Navy or Air Force. The girls are on the land, in the munition factories, in one of the uniformed, auxiliary services. The elders are Air Raid Wardens or Home Guards. They are defenders of the Home Front – a phrase which has a literal meaning for the island of Britain itself is in the front line. Its cities are liable to daily attack, its coasts are rimmed with danger.

To look through these photographs is to recapture successive thrills of the war – the queer unreality of the sunny mornings in September when the ultimatum to Germany expired, the early discomforts of the blackout, the shock and the prompt rally after it that followed the news of Dunkirk, the speed with which a great volunteer army came into being, the brief, intense drama of air battles over Britain, the fantastic scenes in the Tube where tired Londoners sought for sleep, the gallant epic of fire-fighting and rescue in the Blitz.

In addition there is here a panorama of the daily life and doings of the people. They have made Britain into a giant airfield; a vast training ground where the technique of war is learnt; they pile up the munitions in the factories; turn over the land that had never previously known the plough; lay down the keeps of new ships in an unpausing succession.

In days to come many things appearing in these pictures will be of historic interest. It may be that the last word in mechanical progress (as it appeared at the time) in those future days will look rather primitive. As the plane of 1914 was to the giant bomber of the Second World War, so will this be in turn to the 250-seat, round-the-world airliner of to-morrow. The dwellers in replanned cities will look with curious interest at the ruins and smouldering debris, on whch, phœnix-like, new buildings have arisen. At the same time this family album (so indeed it may be called), for never was the nation more closely united, has one thing in it without date – that is the spirit of the British people, who acted, under unprecedented circumstances, just as might be expected from their tradition.

ACTIVITY 15

Front page stories

Collect a copy of three different newspapers. They need not all have been published on the same day, though you may wish to look at papers on the same day for the sake of investigative tidiness.

Together the papers represent a general kind of journalism but you are going to concentrate on front page journalism which, in the case of tabloids, can be minimal in its use of words, but still have all the features of a discourse.

Look at each lead story and write a short description of the kind of reader implied or assumed by the paper. Remember that, up until your eyes were drawn to the first paper, your mind was your own, happily thinking about what it wanted to think about, or doing nothing at all. Once you start to read you are participating in a discourse; you may like it, you may not like it, but most often readers don't even notice because the taking-for-granted principle works so well.

1 What kinds of words are being used? Identify key ones.
2 What contribution does a picture make to your reading? Remember that you 'read' pictures too.
3 What role have you been assigned? How is it expected that you will react?
4 What is the taken-for-granted view of the world? Perhaps it is that people are more interested in the sex lives of celebrities than in anything else.

Discourse and advertising

As readers read a newspaper or magazine they encounter a variety of discourses as their eyes and minds move from news items, to articles, to weather forecasts, to sports reports, to horoscopes, to advertisements. As with headlines, an effective advertisement will tune the reader into its wavelength as quickly as possible.

ACTIVITY 16

Superwaifs

Look at the advertisement opposite and apply the method of analysis used so far:

1 What role is assigned to the reader? What sorts of reactions and responses are expected?
2 What world view is taken for granted or preferred?
3 What kind of information is included? How is it angled?
4 What words, phrases, grammatical features achieve the discourse features you have noticed above?
5 How does the picture contribute to the overall meaning?

- Make sure you give attention to:
- 'superwaif'
- 'impressionable young girls'
- 'and most girls certainly don't'
- 'Of course we can't claim to solve complex problems ...'

6 Why are the 'girls' in the third person?
7 Who is the 'you' in the opening question?

TEXT 13

How do you help girls fed on a diet of this?

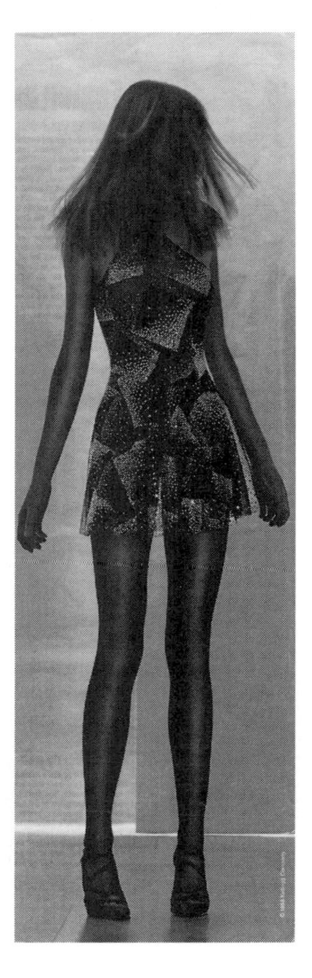

For years every other magazine has been portraying "superwaif" models as the ideal. And impressionable young girls often feel pressure to conform. Which frequently leads them to skip meals like breakfast. And we all know that is hardly the best way to start the day. What you may not know (and most girls certainly don't) is that it has been shown that people who have a good cereal breakfast like Kellogg's tend to maintain a healthier body weight than people who skip breakfast altogether.

This is helped by the body being satisfied early in the day. So there's less likelihood of snacking later on. Also, the body burns off the energy it gets from carbohydrate-rich foods like Kellogg's cereals much more readily than the energy it gets from fatty foods.

Of course, we can't claim to solve complex problems, but we think these are arguments that could help persuade girls to take better care of themselves. And even if they think they're just doing something to say nice and slim, you know they're getting a good nutritious foundation for the day ahead. With the additional benefit of at least ¼ of 6 essential B vitamins and ⅙ of the iron recommended every day. For more information phone Kelloggs' on 0800 626 066.

Kellogg's
Serving the Nation's Health

ACTIVITY 17

Benetton Colours

The following texts are taken from the Internet. The first entries, taken from the *Observer* newspaper (18 February 1996), criticise the Benetton style of advertising; the second piece is by Benetton.

Read the texts and in the light of the arguments, collect some examples of modern advertising that include or address an issue. The Kellogg's advertisement in the previous activity could be seen in this light.

It may take a little time to collect a couple of examples but when you have done so, explore the kind of discourse the advertiser has drawn you into. Write a piece for inclusion on the Internet. Discuss whether you think advertising of this kind is moral.

The advertisements you chose may not contain words. This doesn't matter, but pay very close attention to the words used in the various arguments.

TEXT 14

SOURCE: The Observer DATE: 18 February 1996
Hue and cry over blood-red Benetton
ROGER TREDRE

Third World horror exploited to sell jumpers

One photograph shows a dead African with the top of his head blown off; another the shredded legs of a land mine victim in close-up.

The shocking images appear in full colour in the latest edition of *Colors*, the Benetton magazine, as a statement against war.

Frontline aid agencies, however, have criticised the fashion retail house with a reputation for controversial marketing tactics, claiming the pictures are 'brutalising and gratuitous'.

With the £2 magazine about to go on sale in newsagent and Benetton stores worldwide, Martin Cottingham, a spokesman for Christian Aid, said: 'There is a place for shock tactics, but to put these images in a coffee-table magazine for the shifting of jumpers is totally unjustifiable.'

Geoff Sayer, who runs Oxfam's picture library, said: 'We completely eschew the use of these sort of images.'

Conor Foley, campaigns director of War On Want, warned that the publication of such shocking photographs could make violence seem chic. 'We would not necessarily condemn it, but there is a danger with some of this imagery that it can verge on the pornographic,' he said.

Alex Marashian, editor-in-chief of *Colors*, which is based in Paris, yesterday defended the use of the photographs. 'As we did increasing research on the subject of war, we became amazed at the money spent to create killing technology. We thought it would be dishonest not to confront the issue of what weapons actually do to their victims.'

TEXT 15

SOURCE: The Observer DATE: 07 april 1996
In Brief: Heart ads ban

Sri Jegarajah and Hannah Pool

A Benetton advertisement showing three human hearts has been banned from London Underground stations by managers who felt commuters were too squeamish to face the internal organs first thing in the morning, write Sri Jegarajah and Hannah Pool.

The posters, showing the hearts labelled 'white, black and yellow' with the United Colours of Benetton's logo in the corner, have been blanked out. Benetton defended its campaign arguing that the ad carried a clear anti-racist message – people were all the same inside regardless of colour.

TEXT 16

Communication Policy

Benetton's communication strategy was born of the company's wish to produce images of global concern for its global customers. We realised some time ago that we had a unique tool for communicating worldwide, as we are present in 120 countries, and that it would be cynical to waste it on self-serving product promotion. We trusted in the intelligence of our customers worldwide and decided to give space to issues over redundant product claims.

We have therefore opted for a communication stratgegy in which issues and not clothes, play the lead part. The company has decided to devote some of its advertising budget to communicate on themes relevant to young and old people worldwide. Benetton believes that it is important for companies to take a stance in the real world instead of using their advertising budget to perpetuate the myth that they can make consumers happy through the mere purchase of their product.

Unlike traditional adverts, our images usually have no copy and no product, only our logo. They do not show you a fictitious reality in which you will be irresistible if you make use of our products. They do not tell anyone to buy our clothes, they do not even imply it. All they attempt to do is promote a discussion about issues which people would normally glide over if they approached them from other channels, issues we feel should be more widely discussed.

In so far as our product is concerned, we advertise it through a range of well-placed shops and catalogues, as well as fashion editorials in which our range is displayed directly to the consumer. We have public relations offices in all key countries who liaise with fashion editors. In these instances, we use traditional marketing techniques to ensure our prodcuts get good exposure, good sales personnel, and so forth.

We are aware of the controversy that some of our images have caused, but we believe that all worthwhile stances will have supporters and detractors. Our hope is that people will move from the sterile discussion of whether or not a company is entitled to illustrate its point of view in its advertising campaigns, to a discussion of the issues themselves. In various countries, this has already happened. As more and more people understand our position and the urgency of these issues, we hope to become the vehicle for discussion and not its focus.

So far you have considered different orders of discourse and the assumptions and implied meanings of some examples. In the process you will have developed some ideas of just what discourse is. A summary is provided at the end of the chapter, but turn now to a further exploration of the idea of 'power'.

Power

Dictionaries define 'power' under five general headings:

1 physical
2 scientific/technological
3 mathematical
4 social
5 colloquial and figurative.

For the purpose of this book, the first three definitions can be put to one side. The specific concern here is 'social power'. Notice though how the word 'power' pervades everyday colloquial and figurative expressions:

- a power of good
- power mad
- the powers that be
- power to the people
- power politics.

These are the surest confirmation, if any were needed, of how much we are aware of different kinds of power in our everyday lives.

The *Fontana Dictionary of Modern Thought* (1988) explains how sociologists distinguish between 'social power' as 'authority' and 'physical power' as 'force'. The police, for example, have the power to use 'reasonable force' by virtue of the authority with which the law has empowered them. A consensus of opinion gives power to specific people and institutions who establish and regulate the rules a society lives by. Some rules are informal, others formal. Informal rules are often customary and unwritten, for example, queuing, fair play in sport, common courtesy and fair trading, telling the truth. Much informal language use is interwoven with these behaviour rules. Grice's Maxims, for example (don't talk too much; be truthful; be relevant; be clear) are not a formal rule book but observations of what people intuitively do most of the time. They make for 'sincerity', a highly valued personal quality – everybody knows the difference between accidentally 'breaking a rule' and deliberately flouting it. Formal rules, on the other hand, depend upon language to formulate them, as in laws, statutes, contracts, bills of sale, property deeds, wills and certificates.

Formal Discourse

ACTIVITY 18

This is to certify . . .

For this activity you will benefit from working with two or three other students in order to collect a variety of examples. Look for examples of documents that embody formal rules and authority. Here are some examples:

- GCSE certificates;
- hire purchase agreement;
- bus pass;
- a five pound note;
- a college/student contract;
- a birth certificate;
- any legal document;
- a doctor's note;
- a coursework cover sheet.

Look at the language first and identify the words and phrases that signify the power or authority of the text. Authority may be signalled by a verb: 'This certifies that ...', a signature, a promise or any combination of such things. Note too that documents of this kind possess an instrumental power: they prove something, enable you to do something, go somewhere or get in. Lose them, fail to sign them, let them get out of date, and if not actually in trouble, you will be in for a certain amount of inconvenience.

The combination of authority, force, formal laws and social conventions binds society together. It keeps us secure, in a state of 'law and order'. By and large, we assent and conform. It structures the way in which we think as well as behave. It constructs in our minds a value system and it does this through language, and particularly through different kinds of discourse. The possession of wealth, specialist knowledge and control of, or strong influence in, media and communications, make it possible to manipulate and exploit conformity.

Discourse in protest

Language uses, on the one hand, reinforce power structures, the strength of social convention and public morality, but, on the other hand, they can also question and protest. The latter is a language function very much in evidence in the latter part of the 20th century.

A famous literary example of language being used to control the way its users think is George Orwell's *1984* (published in 1948) in which the Ministry for War, for example, is named the Ministry for Peace whilst retaining the prime function of making war.

Re-naming jobs and even renumbering rooms is a familiar strategy whereby 'new management' makes its mark on an existing organisation. In fact, the power to decide on what things shall be called is a considerable one in any walk of life. The invention of the name 'Greenpeace' is a very notable example, as indeed was the naming of the ship 'Rainbow Warrior'.

David Crystal points out incidentally that, very early in life, children learn the language of resistance and protest. Up to the age of seven, they use the word 'No' eight times more frequently than adults.

ACTIVITY 19

The writing on the wall

An ancient form of protest is the writing of graffiti in public places. Graffiti often amuse, sometimes sicken and horrify, occasionally bewilder. They are ways of questioning the status quo, expressing dissent, subverting the system.

Collect examples of graffiti over a period of a week or two and identify what it is that is being questioned or attacked. Note if they are statements, exclamations, questions or imperatives. Note also their emotional force and any humour. Are any incomprehensible to you?

Slogans

You know it makes sense

Slogans are phrases made to promote a product, a cause or an idea. Advertisers can make fortunes out of slogans, political parties have always depended on them, consumer products can sell in millions because of them. Large sums of money are invested in their invention and their hoped-for memorability, yet they are relatively short-lived in the media though they often linger in the mind: 'He were a great baker, our dad'.

Some familiar examples from government sources are:

- Clunk, Click, Every Trip
- Don't Drink and Drive
- Join the Professionals
- Keep Britain Tidy

- Save It
- Watch Out, There's a Thief About
- You Know It Makes Sense
- Your Country Needs You
- Careless Talk Costs Lives.

Commercial advertising slogans from an earlier age include:

- My goodness, My Guinness
- Go To Work on an Egg
- You Can Be Sure of Shell
- Player's Please
- It Beats as it Sweeps as it Cleans
- Drink Tizer the Appetizer
- Eat More Fruit
- Happiness is a Cigar called Hamlet
- Beanz Meanz Heinz
- Have A Break, Have a Kit Kat.

ACTIVITY 20

A more recent example would be, 'Because I'm Worth It' (L'Oreal). Lots of discourse implications in this one:

1 What role does it assign the reader? (Identification? Approval of self worth?)
2 What values or world view lie behind it?
3 What is taken for granted?
4 What are the key words and grammatical points?

Look at some modern commercial and political slogans. Try Macdonalds, Coca Cola, Calvin Klein and the political and paramilitary groups of Northern Ireland.
For each example, note if a verb is used and examine the sentence type (imperative, statement). Ask yourself what are the values lying behind it and what assumption is made about you the reader.

COMMENTARY

The data you have collected in the previous two activities contrasts in an interesting way. One set of data is largely about protest, the other about promotion, two different kinds of discourse. If you looked at each systematically you should have gained a view on different roles assigned to you. Coca Cola assumes that you are/want to be thought of as a globally minded, non-racist person. You should also have gained insights into assumed values and preferred, taken-for-granted points of view, for instance that multinational advertising not only promotes products and profits, but also peace and harmony.

The aim in this chapter is not to paint a picture of a greedy society, locked in a malignant, conspiratorial struggle of winners and losers, the powerful and the powerless, the exploiting profiteers and politicians and the exploited, duped general public. The main concern is to help you investigate the society you live in through the texts it generates, and to concentrate particularly on expressions and reflections of social power in and behind those texts. Look finally at two examples of charity advertising.

Discourse and charities

ACTIVITY 21

Changing the way people think

Of course charities are always asking for money. They cannot function without it. It's a truism therefore to say that all their advertising is begging. But that would be cynical and the word 'begging' is a loaded term. (Ask the two questions that should by now be familiar: What role does the use of the word assign to me? What values/view of the world lie behind it?)

The two advertisements below appeared on hoardings in the streets and in newspapers and magazines.

Read them taking note of the grammatical constructions in particular. Explain what kind of discourse the adverts represent by relating their grammatical features to the role of the reader and the implied meanings and values. What is the purpose behind them since they do not explicitly ask for money?

TEXT 17

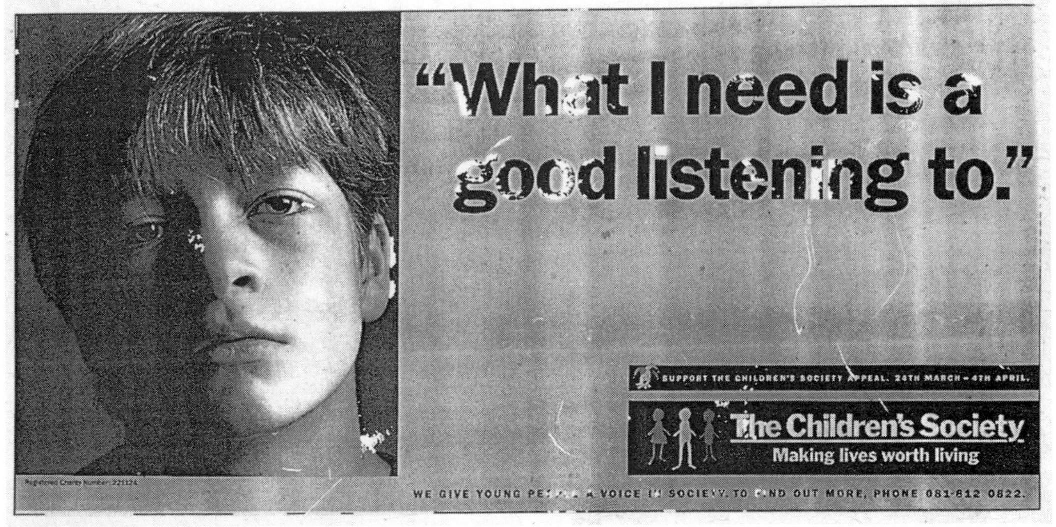

COMMENTARY

In Text 17, some significant details are :

- 'What I need is . . .'
- '. . .a () listening to . . .'
- '. . .give a voice . . .'

Here is an organisation of considerable moral influence, though much less political and financial power, trying to change an attitude of mind. It is not asking for money. This change of mind is brought about by challenging habitual language use. We live in a culture where adults are more likely to say of young people: 'They need a good talking to.' The advertisement reverses expectations: want/need, talking to/listening to. It also echoes but questions a Victorian ideal that children should be seen but not heard. Note too that the Children's Society who produced the poster, present the organisation as spokespersons. The verb 'give' implies a powerlessness (they won't be heard) on the part of the children in question. Giving people a voice is a remarkable action when we take for granted that people can speak or speak up for themselves. It is worth noting that this advertisement

TEXT 18

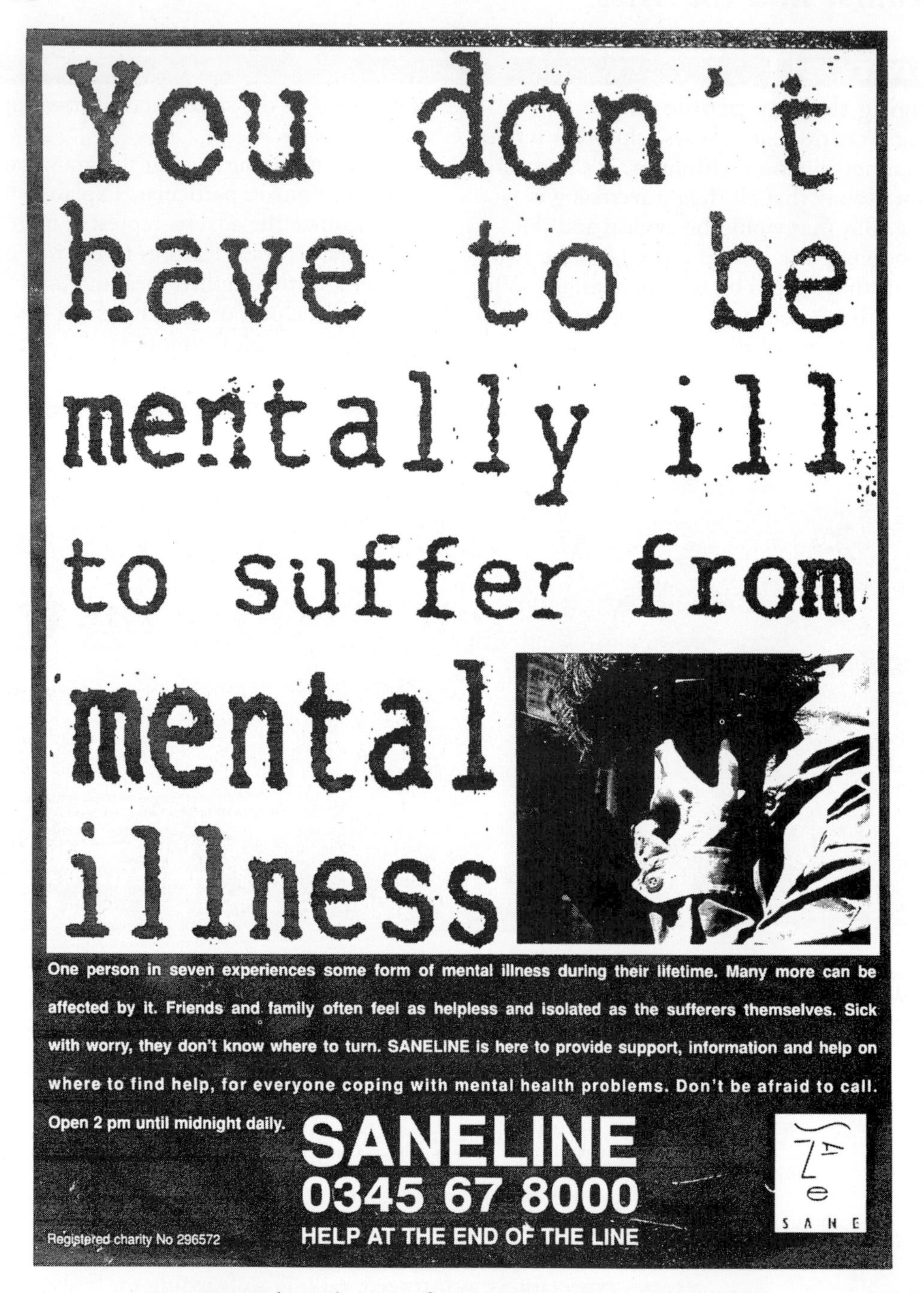

appeared on the eve of a new national awareness of the extent of child abuse and neglect, hitherto unheeded.

The use of 'What I need . . .' as a sentence opener is worth looking at. Other forms are, 'What we need . . .', 'What I think is . . .', 'What gets me is . . .'. 'What I want to know is . . .'. Tony Blair, the Labour Prime Minister frequently uses similar constructions to preface things he is saying in public interviews: 'What I would say to you is this . . .'. Other politicians use it too. Notice the introduction of a modal verb (would) not used in the advert, which makes an interesting construction all the more intriguing. Modal verbs often convey hedging but prefacing your remarks with 'What I would say is this . . .' expresses both an awareness of the importance of your pronouncements together with a caution about future implications. In the Children's Society advert the effect of this construction is even more emphatic for *not* containing a modal. It is a strong plea to be heard.

With Text 18 the organisation SANE wants to change attitudes towards mental health. It focuses on people who are caring for someone who has suffered or is suffering from mental illness – the 'you' at the beginning of the sentence. It recognises that carers suffer consequences from caring. The 'you' are quietly desperate people who themselves need care and advice. or a voice perhaps, as in the previous advert. But lying behind the advertisement are long standing attitudes to mental illness that also need to be changed.

The French thinker, Michel Foucault, has explored the way in which people have treated and talked about mental illness (*Madness and Civilisation – a History of Insanity in the Age of Reason*, Routledge, 1990). His concern is not just how it is talked about but also how it is imagined. In one age madness was a spectacle, in another it was confined to asylums while in more recent times it is treated as an illness.

Mental illness has long been thought of as a person's complete identity. It possesses the whole being and as such is frightening, possibly hopeless. It is rather like having a habit of expression that says to the physically sick, 'You *are* diseased', instead of the more usual, 'You've *got* 'flu'. The use of a form of the verb 'to be' in the first half of the sentence refers to a state whereas in the second half, mental illness is presented as a 'thing' that comes from outside and afflicts you like flu. The word 'from' separates the illness from the victim as though it were flu, toothache, measles or a bad back.

However you interpret these advertisements, they are both trying to change ways in which people think, to change prevailing ideologies. There is a school of stylistic analysis called 'Critical Linguistics' (see *Literature as Social Discourse*, by Roger Fowler, Batsford, 1989). This school holds that no discourse is innocent, transparent or neutral. All discourses reflect ideological assumptions.

Ideology

Ideology is one of those words that can be frightening, mystifying, meaningless, even boring because it is so abstract. Possibly it is coming to the end of a long and good life. For many, the word signifies political 'isms': Socialism, Fascism, Stalinism, Conservatism, Imperialism. Linguistically speaking it means 'idea words': words used to express abstract ideas which are nevertheless very motivating; ideas of how people live their lives and act out their attitudes. You do not need to use the word if you don't like it, though many linguists still find it essential. It is a convenient term for expressing collectively many of the phrases used in this chapter: belief system, ideas, underlying assumptions, world view, taken-for-grantedness, values. How ideologies are constructed in texts is one key purpose of stylistics and turns mere feature spotting into something more interesting and useful. Do remember though that ideologies are not necessarily political. In addition to ideological issues to do with war, you have also encountered other ideologies to do with eating and appearance, child care, mental illness, advertising slogans.

Throughout the book you will encounter texts with other ideologies. One way of looking at, for want of a better term, everyday ideologies is to explore some of the differences of opinion you have with an otherwise good friend. It may be to do with eating meat, smoking, politics or religion. The latter two are traditionally regarded as no-go areas if you just want polite, friendly conversation. This, in itself, tells you how deep ideologies lie in discourse.

This chapter has explored the idea of discourse and investigated texts in different discourses:

- varieties of family talk
- readers' letters
- reporting the Gulf War
- front page stories
- Kellogg's and Benetton advertising
- graffiti
- slogans
- charity advertising.

The notion of 'power' was further explored in terms of authority and the way in which discourse structures tend to support prevailing social structures and embody dominant values assumptions, belief systems and attitudes. Some texts however attempt to change ways in which people think. Two aspects of discourse that are need to be identified are:

- the role assigned to the reader by a text
- the underlying assumptions, values and world view of a text.

By means of stylistic analysis, these intuitions can be demonstrated by references to lexical and grammatical choices in the text. Attention to what names are given to items or persons in a text will reveal attitudes: 'ethnic cleansing' as a euphemism for 'massacre'. Choice of adverbs and adjectives also encode attitudes. Similarly verbs that evaluate, use modals or express existence/possession give further clues to authorial point of view and contribute to the tone of a text. Another word for all these strands that can be detected in a text by a critical reader is ideology.

3 Lifestylistics: Language, Power and Culture

The term 'Discourse' points to connections between social power and language as realised in texts. This chapter is concerned with connections between language and society in terms of the cultures in which we live.

You will explore the word 'culture' and then consider a modern equivalent, 'lifestyle'. Other issues raised will be consumerism and communication media. The textual focus will be mainly on polemical texts about business organisation, television and the arts.

Culture

The word 'culture' is a difficult one to drop into an everyday conversation. It can sound pompous, off-putting, embarrassing, even downright snobbish. When did you last use the word?

Most frequently it is associated with classical music, fine arts, good books and expensive tastes. It's a poker-faced sort of word, almost always used in serious contexts.

The terms 'high brow', 'middle brow' and 'low brow' used to be used to describe different levels of cultural interest. There were even 'no brows'! As with dialect and accent, culture is a topic littered with stereotypes.

The word is ordinary enough in its Latin origin. It occurs for example in words like 'agriculture' and 'horticulture'. People use these words quite happily. The word is also related to the word 'manure', derived from Middle English 'manouren', meaning 'to till' or 'to cultivate' soil. You couldn't get more down to earth than that! And yet the word is most often taken to mean something airy-fairy, high falutin, posh and arty. The Victorian poet and among other things, schools inspector, Matthew Arnold, wrote a book contrasting 'culture' with 'anarchy' (*Culture and Anarchy*, 1869). For him, culture was the pursuit of 'sweetness and light'. To some modern readers, that may sound effete now. Certainly it was not the view of the Nazi, Hermann Goering: 'When I hear anyone talk of culture, I reach for my revolver'. He also said in a 1936 German radio broadcast: 'Guns will make us powerful; butter will make us fat'.

ACTIVITY 22

Culture

It is always useful to take a lexicographical look at a word with such a long history.

First take a diachronic look. Using the biggest dictionary you can find, check the origin of the word and its various meanings over the years. If you have access to the *Oxford English Dictionary* on CD-Rom, all the better.

Make a note of the meanings you have discovered and write down other words in the word family, for example, cult, cultivated, cultured.

Write down some sentences in which the words could occur:

- She is a very cultivated person.
- He cultivates important people.
- They belong to entirely different cultures.

Now take a synchronic approach – this is explained below. To do this you will not need a dictionary, but the help of other people.

An ongoing approach would be to scan newspapers and magazines and to note things overheard, but this takes time. A more direct approach to get at synchronic meanings (how people use the word now) is to ask people questions and to note down their responses:

- Who is the most cultured person you know, and why?
- What does the word 'culture' mean to you?

You may get the answer, 'Not a lot', to the last question, but if you ask ten people you should be able to get an idea about any popular meaning the word has today. Make sure you record the age, gender and occupation of your subjects.

Compare your ten responses with those of other students. See what people say and remember, be objective. Your data is valid synchronic data. You may need to revise your questions to get fuller responses a second time.

COMMENTARY

You may have found that some people think of culture as belonging to an earlier age that contrasts with modern times. Others may associate the word with social class, art galleries and being intellectual. Here are some contrasts discovered by one group of students:

high class	low class
country	town
then	now
educated	uneducated
arts	sciences
spiritual values	material values
good taste	bad taste
refinement	vulgarity

Whatever view you take of culture in a historical or popular sense, there are two related areas in which the word has taken on a new and vigorous lease of life: managememt in business organisations and public sector administration.

Business Culture

ACTIVITY 23

Disney World

The following texts are taken from highly respected books on the management of organisations. Text 19 is from *In Search of Excellence* by Thomas J. Peters and Robert H. Waterman Jr (Harper Collins, 1982). Text 20 is from *Organisational Behaviour* by Andrzej Huczynski and David Buchanan (Prentice Hall, 1985)

TEXT 19

The Importance of Culture

Some colleagues who have heard us expound on the importance of values and distinctive cultures have said in effect, "That's swell, but isn't it a luxury? Doesn't the business have to make money first?" The answer is that, of course, a business has to be fiscally sound. And the excellent companies are among the most fiscally sound of all. But their value set *integrates* the notions of economic health, serving customers, and making meanings down the line. As one executive said to us, "Profit is like health. You need it, and the more the better. But it's not why you exist." Moreover, in a piece of research that preceded this work, we found that companies whose only articulated goals were financial did not do nearly as well financially as companies that had broader sets of values.

Yet it's surprising how little is said about the shaping of values in current management theories – particularly how little is said about companies as cultures. ...

Andrew Pettigrew sees the process of shaping culture as the prime management role: "The [leader] not only creates the rational and tangible aspects of organizations, such as structure and technology, but also is the creator of symbols, ideologies, language beliefs, rituals, and myths." Using strikingly similar language, Joanne Martin of Stanford thinks of organizations as "systems composed of ideas, the meaning of which must be managed." Martin has spurred a great deal of practical, specific research that indicates the degree to which rich networks of legends and parables of all sorts pervade top-performing institutions. HP, IBM, and DEC are three of her favourite examples. The research also indicates that the poor performers are relatively barren in this dimension. Warren Bennis also speaks of the primacy of image and metaphor:

"It is not so much the articulation of goals about what an [institution] *should* be doing that creates new practice. It's the imagery that creates the understanding ... Thus, if I were to give off-the-cuff advice to anyone trying to institute change, I would say, "How clear is the metaphor? How is that understood? How much energy are you devoting to it?"

... people are encouraged to stick out, to innovate. Thus, "IBM Means Service" underscores the company's overpowering devotion to the individual customer; but that very formulation also provides remarkable space. Everyone, from clerks on up, is prodded to do whatever he or she can think of to ensure that the individual customer gets taken care of. In a more mundane setting, Steven Rothman, writing in *D&B Reports*, quotes a Tupperware dealer: "The company gives me great freedom to develop my own approach. There are certain elements that need to be in every party to make it successful, but if those elements are colored by you, a Tupperware dealer – purple, pink and polka dot, and I prefer it lavender and lace – that's okay. That freedom allows you to be the best you are capable of being." So, in fact, the power of the value is in large measure that it encourages practical innovation to carry out its spirit to the full.

1. Look first at Text 19 and write, in 50 or so of your own words exactly what Peters and Waterman mean by 'values and distinctive cultures'.
2. Make a list of the kinds of language use discussed eg myths that construct and transmit organisational cultures.
3. How important do you think spoken language is in creating a culture? Deduce examples from the text.

Now read Text 20, which consists of linked excerpts from Huczynski and Buchanan.

1 Write in about 50 words a description of 'corporate culture' as seen here.
2 List all the ways cited in which language plays a part in creating and sustaining corporate culture.
3 Look at the Mickey Mouse Culture inset and relate this to the headings from Trice and Beyer cited in the text.
4 How spontaneous, democratic and popular do you find the ideas of culture presented here, and how far do you consider it a form of manipulation and exploitation?

TEXT 20

Corporate culture

During the 1980s a great deal of attention began to be paid in management studies to the concept of company or *corporate culture.*

Definition

Culture is 'the system of ... publicly and collectively accepted meanings operating for a given group at a given time.'

... Culture helps organizational members to interpret their world and publicly accept it despite any reservations that they may have.

Trice and Beyer (1984) detailed the elements which constitute the culture of an organization. They grouped these under the headings of company practices, company communications, physical cultural forms and common language.

Huczynski and Buchanan conveniently summarise the work of Trice and Beyer in the excerpts below. Read them and do the tasks which follow.

Company practices

1. *Rite* This is a planned, and often a dramatic activity which was elaborately staged and which focused different expressions of culture into a single event. A wedding ceremony or a 'Suggestion Scheme Winner of the Year' award ceremony are examples of rites.
2. *Ceremonial* This involves a linked series of rites within a single event. An occasion which included the ceremonial unveiling of a product, the honouring of employees' extraordinary work performance, and the hearing of visions of the future from an inspirational leader would rate as a ceremonial.
3. *Ritual* These are standardised techniques which, while they may manage anxieties, do not produce practical consequences of any importance.

American companies arrange regular Friday afternoon 'beer busts' at which workers can get together and relax. The Digital Equipment Company (DEC) in Scotland holds regular plant barbeques with free drinks, to encourage staff at all levels and from different functions to mix socially.

Company communications

Trice and Beyer itemised the ways in which organisation members typically communicated and expressed themselves as representing elements of culture.

4. *Stories* Based on original true events, but now include both truth and fiction. For example, the story of the employee who noticed that the labels on a P&G product at his local supermarket were mounted off centre. He bought the whole stock assuming P&G would reimburse him, which they did.
5. *Myths* These are stories which lack a factual basis and which often include old-timers' stories of things that happened in the past.
6. *Sagas* Historical narratives describing the unique accomplishments of a group and its leaders. For example, Hewlett Packard sagas of the accomplishments of Bill (Hewlett) and Dave (Packard) are used to communucate features of the 'H-P Way'.
7. *Legends* Accounts of actual events which have been embellished with fictional details. The legends frequently concern individuals as heroes and heroines. For example, the 3M legend of the worker who persistently tried to find a way to use rejected sandpaper minerals. He was fired for spending time on this, kept coming back, and was ultimately successful, becoming the Vice-President of the company's Roofing Granuals Division which he helped to create.
8. *Folk tales* Purely fictional stories which nevertheless carry a message for employee behaviour and practice.
9. *Symbols and slogans* Examples of symbols include the Coca Cola and IBM logos. Slogans such as Caterpillar's 'Forty-eight hour parts service anywhere in the world' or 'I Think Therefore IBM' are well known.

Physical cultural forms

These may be material goods or physical environments.

10. *Artifacts* Tools, furniture and appliances. For example, it is claimed that every IBM office has a flipchart.
11. *Physical layout* Buildings, open spaces and office layouts. For example, the replacement of four-seater tables in a canteen by six-seater ones to increase the chances of employees from different departments meeting and interacting with each other.

Common language

A number of companies do not have 'workers'. Wal-mart has 'associates', and McDonald's has 'crew members'. Companies also have modes of internal communication which convey their own meanings. Thus for example, Procter and Gamble have the 'one page memorandum' rule.

Mickey Mouse culture

Marne-la-Vallée is situated 26 kilometres east of Paris and has been chosen by the Walt Disney Corporation as the location for its first European theme park. The responsibility for the initial communication of the company's corporate culture lies with the local Disney University (company training centre). This is under the direction of Mary Toedt who has been with the corporation for twenty years. The purpose of the training is to:

1. Familiarize new employees with the Disney tradition and operating philiosophy.
2. Teach them Walt Disney's vision by giving them a history of the company from its beginnings through to the death of its founder.
3. Familiarize them with Disneyland language. The operation is a *show*, the customers are *Guests* (spelled with a capital G); the collective workforce is the *cast;* individual employees are *hosts;* and working with the public involves being on *stage.*
4. Provide them with an understanding of the Euro Disneyland ethos, teaching them acting and 'atmospherics'.
5. Develop generic skills to be used on Guests such as smiling and answering questions.
6. Developing job specific skills such as sweeping up, answering the telephone and attending the car park.

Toedt reported that her French recruits were more reserved than their American counterparts but had, nevertheless, been transformed. Gillet reported that some of these new entrants had withdrawn from the training complaining that, 'Joining the Disney organization is a bit like taking holy orders or, in the opinion of more recalcitrant candidates, joining a sect'.

Based on Anne Gillet, 'Mickey Mouse goes to France', *Tertiel,* May 1989. Reprinted in *Best of Business,* 1990, vol 2, no. 1, pp. 28–33.

COMMENTARY

You will understand the importance of language for sustaining and promoting corporate values and company power structures in a particular cultural style. Note how important fictions of different kinds are and the recognition of the power of metaphor and imagination. In order to understand the principles set out here, you could look at your own school or college in terms of its corporate culture. Focus your attention on the linguistic evidence for the practices identified by Trice and Beyer. How many apply?

Lifestyle and culture

The word 'Lifestyle', an abstract, compound noun, is in a number of ways a modern version of the word 'culture'. It is a comprehensive word, covering the whole of life rather than just work as in the previous texts. Sociologists and anthropologists use the word 'culture' as an abstract noun covering the languages, customs, beliefs, conventions and varieties of social behaviour observable in any human society. This chapter is concerned with the kinds of language data and texts that provide evidence of how we live now, inside our heads as well as in our social behaviour. The word 'lifestyle' became popular in the 1960s and is now a term frequently used to refer to cultural activities like leisure pursuits, income bracket, level of education, food preferences, love relationships, reading habits, clothes and financial priorities.

ACTIVITY 24

Lifestyle

The booksellers, W. H. Smith, use the term as a shelf title to classify certain types of magazine. Visit a branch, preferably a large one, and note down the magazines classified under lifestyle. Make a note of titles and also the kinds of language featured on the front cover. These words are usually superimposed on a picture.

1 What idea of lifestyle would an English reading alien get from this kind of evidence?
2 A complete range of magazines, not just lifestyle titles, provides an interesting index to the variety of cultural interests of large numbers of people. Study a range, and note the relatively small number of magazines, maybe only one, bought by each individual.
3 Observe too, who buys what, their age and gender group. If you stay long enough you will begin to 'read' patterns of magazine choice. Include people who stand and read magazines without actually buying them, a regular occurrence among W. H. Smith customers.

ACTIVITY 25

A matter of taste

Write lifestyle profiles of two or three people you know. Include what you know or believe about their values and attitudes as well as what they actually do with their leisure time. You will need to take into account their work or their studies. Economic factors are very important to culture.

What would you say were the main linguistic influences on their lifestyle? Talk (with whom, when, where?); TV (which programmes?); books (what kind?); newspapers and magazines?; film?

So far you have looked at lifestyle, culture, the way we live now, call it what you will, as a mainstream part of human society – how we live, work, spend and take time off. No doubt you will be aware of alternative lifestyles ranging from subsistence gardening and no TV, to a down and (not necessarily) out life on the street.

Read the following text and identify and describe:

1 The language strategies used by the writer.
2 Your own reactions. Ask, for example, what role is assigned to you the reader, and what world view, values, ideology underlie the text.

TEXT 21

Choose life. Choose a job. Choose a career. Choose a family. Choose a fucking big television, choose washing machines, cars, compact disc players and electrical tin openers. Choose good health, low cholesterol, and dental insurance. Choose fixed interest mortgage repayments. Choose your friends. Choose leisurewear and matching luggage. Choose a three piece suite on hire purchase in a range of fucking fabrics. Choose DIY and wondering who the fuck you are on a Sunday morning. Choose sitting on that couch watching mind-numbing, spirit-crushing game shows, stuffing fucking junk food into your mouth. Choose rotting away at the end of it all, pishing your last in a miserable home, nothing more than an embarrassment to the selfish, fucked up brats you spawned to replace yourself. CHOOSE YOUR FUTURE. CHOOSE LIFE.

Trainspotting, Irvine Welsh (1995).

COMMENTARY

- The style of the text is uncompromisingly imperative yet ironic. Note the repetitions and the lists, first of consumer goods, then of domestic activities. A lifestyle here is raged against, scorched by the words. It is an extreme polemic against a way of life.
- Do you detect any positive values? What could 'Choose life' mean? How does it compare with similar modern sayings such as 'Get a life' and 'Get real'? German sociologists traditionally distinguish between 'culture' and 'civilisation'. 'Culture' (Kultur) is a matter of spiritual and personal values; civilisation is a matter of material values and the masses. The text here attacks material civilisation rather than culture.
- Write a companion to this text which itemises and celebrates the kind of life and values that might be chosen as an alternative.
- Specifically, the polemic in this text is against consumerism as a way of life that is ultimately meaningless. The word 'polemic' comes from the Greek 'polemikos' meaning 'warlike'. Good polemical writing is argument that is controversial, deeply felt yet controlled, and aimed at promoting greater awareness and responsive action. It must be well argued, though you are not obliged to agree: it often makes lively reading, especially when you don't agree. Sometimes it is angry, abusive, aggressive, pulling no punches; sometimes inspiring.

One characteristic of polemical writing is the way in which writers have the confidence, the nerve, the cheek to speak on behalf of other people, sure in the knowledge that they know what is best or what is wrong. Everytime you talk to friends in that 'putting the world to rights' mood, you are being polemical. A good deal of what is published in newspapers and magazines and broadcast on TV is polemical, very persuasive and easily consumed and backed by powerful influences. The debate about power in and over communications media has been going on for a long time.

Polemical writing

ACTIVITY 26

Servile contentment

Read first a summary of an argument published by Denys Thompson in *Discrimination and Popular Culture* (1970):

Communications media are big business and have developed a life and power of their own. Media production is expensive and must show a profit. Quantity becomes more important than quality, and poor quality is concealed by dazzlingly efficient presentation. To make a profit, media must appeal to consumers; what is presented must be safe, unprovocative, predictable and will aim for the lowest common denominator.

Media controllers have little contact with consumers and ratings are in any case more important than people, just as entertainment is more important than education. High ratings are not necessarily indicative of what consumers want but of efficient product publicity and marketing.

In support of this polemic, Thompson reminds readers of the words of Cecil King, then Chairman of *Daily Mirror* Newspapers:

'In point of fact it is only the people who conduct newspapers and similar organisations who have any idea quite how indifferent, quite how stupid, quite how uninterested in education of any kind the great bulk of the British public are.'

Thompson adds:

'The nineteenth century maimed and enslaved the worker's body; perhaps in the twentieth century it is his mind that is maintained in servile contentment.'

Polemical stuff indeed! First of all, take note of the key terms used and get clear in your own mind what they mean. Don't use a dictionary, decide what they mean in practical terms to you today. Consider: consumers, media production, communications, education.

Next, think about Cecil King's words and Thompson's notion of 'servile contentment' (think also about *Trainspotting*) and assess the truth or value of these opinions as applied to you.

Finally, write about your own point of view (about 200 words) for a new polemical magazine called *Media Rage!*.

Polemical writing often features in A-Level examination papers because of its intrinsic interest or topicality and because of its lively use of language. It is a fascinating kind of discourse in which one ideology is locked in combat with another. This makes it even more important to be able to discern 'where a text is coming from' to use a popular modern phrase that well describes an important aspect of discourse analysis.

You are now going to look at a series of texts on mainly media topics. They will enable you to explore further the themes raised so far: consumerism, entertainment versus education, power and control in the media.

ACTIVITY 27

Carry on repeating

The following article comes from the *Radio Times* (14 February, 1998). It is written by a regular contributor to the Review section in a magazine that clearly assumes that its readers want something more than a list of programme times. There are a number of interesting linguistic issues raised by this piece of polemical writing:

1 What is the purpose of the article?

2 What kind of reader response seems to be anticipated?
3 What role does it assign to you the reader?
4 What does the archaeological scenario give to the article? (Note: Howard Carter discovered the tomb of Tutankhamun in 1922, and a series of programmes on Ancient Egypt had recently been shown.)
5 How do the views and the personality of the writer come across?

TEXT 22

The sitcom tombs best left undisturbed

Howard Carter wiped the sweat from his brow as he prised open the last chamber of the Tomb of the Seventies. This was the final, glorious prize in his excavation of the Valley of the Television Archives. He struggled to break open that final door. He worked diligently and with purpose – he knew there were untold treaures in that dank tomb, which had lain undisturbed for many, many years.

Others had made tentative raids on the Tomb of the Eighties, which had yielded **BRIDESHEAD REVISITED** for Channel 4 (*Saturdays*). But Carter knew the time was right. Terrestrial television was in the doldrums, there was little choice but to unearth some of the great glories of another age and to bring them to the attention of a world desperate for nostalgia.

At last the door gave way. Carter looked around in wonder, as the spirit of the decade swirled around him. The walls were lined with posters of the Bay City Rollers and the Osmonds, whose teeth miraculously appeared to glow in the dark. And could he really hear the strains of *Billy Don't Be a Hero* or had he just had too much sun? He gazed on the accessories buried with the gods and goddesses of TV. Polyester flares, platform shoes, *Starsky and Hutch* belted cardigans, large collars and even bigger ties.

Carter stumbled through the pitiful glow shed by lighted candles in Mateus Rosé bottles and entered the great inner sanctum. He gasped. Rumours of great buried television treasures of the seventies had swirled around the industry for years. But nobody had bothered with an expedition until Carter. And here he was, at last.

Carter bent down and blew the dust of countless years from a sarcophagus. He could make out the words **ARE YOU BEING SERVED?** (*Saturdays BBC1, not Wales*) – 64 episodes, first broadcast 1973. With a recklessness born of the joy of discovery, he broke the seal and the ghosts echoed around the chamber. First a woman's voice: "Getting up so early plays havoc with my pussy." Then a man's (at least, he thought it was a man's): "I'm free." Carter stumbled in horror. Oh no, he had given a new lease of life to outrageous camp and cheap innuendo. He had heard that the Tomb of the Seventies carried a curse. Could this be it? Had he unleashed something so truly hideous on the world, something that would attact millions of viewers on a Saturday teatime?

Carter decided he had to persevere. Surely it could not get any worse than this? Surely there were no other terrors waiting to be rediscovered? He was wrong. The seventies situation comedy chamber was bulging with untold terrors: *Love Thy Neighbour, My Wife Next Door, Bless This House, The Fenn Street Gang.* Carter reeled in disbelief, before running from the chamber and resealing the door. It was too late for *Are You Being Served?* but these others must be left undisturbed, their dreadfulness contained for ever.

Carter crawled towards the ultimate prize he knew was lurking in the great central chamber of seventies icons. He knew some of what he was about to find had been reincarnated. Basil Brush and *The Wombles* were being remade and brought back to TV in the nineties. There was even a new version of *The Professionals* in the pipeline.

But Carter was an optimistic man. He wanted to see the resurrection – not the remaking – of *The Brothers,* one of the great Sunday-night drama serials of all time, and *Within These Walls*, with Googie Withers as the governor of a women's prison. There was still time, the public's appetite for the seventies was unabated. After all, *The Sweeney* had been doing well on Channel 5. Didn't that pave the way for the return of *Shoestring* and *Tinker, Tailor, Soldier, Spy,* which no one understood the first time round?

He crawled towards his prize, passing the sarcophagus of Dave Allen. He opened this instantly and Allen popped out to front his old sketches in a series of compilations, *The Unique Dave Allen*, on BBC1.

Breaking through to the inner chamber, Carter stopped and stared. It was so beautifully preserved. Time appeared to have enhanced, rather than diminished, what he saw in front of him. The blue eyes sparkled, the finely chiselled features glowed with bonhomie. Here was the greatest seventies treasure of them all – Michael Parkinson.

Carter felt a strange compulsion. Suddenly he spoke of his life and his hopes. Something about the man invited confidences. **PARKINSON** (*Fridays BBC1*) listened and smiled. It was good to be back . . . '*RT*'

COMMENTARY

Being entertaining is such an important motive in this text that it is difficult to define its purpose beyond that. Could the answer lie in the final adulatory words about Michael Parkinson, which introduces at the last minute a completely new theme? If the purpose is a critical one (which you would reasonably expect from a review), the writer seems to go for a fairly safe target (seventies sitcoms that date so easily). Elsewhere the criticism seems ambivalent – is she being critical or not? Notice the use of rhetorical questions with an adverb that do not make a direct critical statement but do cast aspersions: 'Surely there were no other terrors . . .' and 'could he really hear the strains of *Billy Don't Be A Hero . . .*' and 'Had he unleashed something so truly hideous . . .'. Mock emotion is all part of the put-down. Notice too, the use of italics for some programmes mentioned and bold print for the ones actually being repeated.

The subtext is about the value of repeats, necessary as a part of commodity profitability, yet they seem to need justifying to an audience always looking for something new. There is a recognition that many readers will welcome the return of *Are You Being Served?* yet a suggestion that they ought not to like its 'outrageous camp and cheap innuendo'. Any verbal comments however are outweighed by the inclusion of a picture (the only picture – not reproduced) of the offending programme.

The build up of the article to the writer's main enthusiasm, Michael Parkinson, confidently assumes that readers will equally welcome his return.

Given that the article appears on the same page as the ratings figures, are the criticisms voiced actually based on the ratings? If you look at the language used, it might well appear so: 'The Sweeney had been doing very well on Channel Four', 'millions of viewers'. Where exactly does the reader stand in relation to 'the millions' and 'the public'? Does the author appear to include herself among them? Is the reader being invited to share a position of knowing superiority with the writer?

The archaeological scenario is clever. It is an example of intertextuality that almost entirely overwhelms the content of the writer's own text. It does in fact account for most of the entertainment which seems to be the writer's main purpose. It generates a style of writing that has an intriguing narrative with mock suspense, whilst at the same time being an amusing way of arguing a point. There is a strong tendency to exaggerate: 'great glories', 'desperate for nostalgia', 'miraculously appeared', 'bulging', 'recklessness'.

How far may the article be said to be maintaining interest in a product even when the product is being recycled as nostalgia?

How far is it disarming criticism by taking an, albeit safe, critical stance of its own? Notice that nostalgia has now become a commodity that has its own section in record and video shops.

ACTIVITY 28

Dumb . . .

The text below also comes from the *Radio Times* (5 July, 1997), Look at 'Whose News Do You Use?' by Steve Clarke. Read the article and summarise in your own words what kind of power news programme producers and editors possess over the presentation of news. What are your responses to the views expressed in the inset boxes, and to the final comment by Richard Tait? Make sure you identify who said what: there is more than one voice in this text.

1 Behind the text, is there an implied view of how news should be handled?
2 Language is very good for setting up persuasive contrasts. What contrasts are set up here?
3 What is the point of the title?

TEXT 23

WHOSE NEWS DO YOU USE?

Here are the headlines. The future of TV news is under threat – a plague of "dumbing down" is revealed in this week's edtion of BBC2's history of TV reportage. Steve Clarke investigates

British television news is poised on the threshold of a revolution. In a decade's time it is possible that today's sober style of news programme, typified by a straight-faced Michael Buerk or Trevor McDonald reading a resumé of the day's key events, will look as anachronistic as a BBC announcer in the fifties, bringing the latest tidings from Westminster in full evening dress.

"News is changing faster than any other area of broadcasting," says Tony Hall, chief executive of BBC News. "It is essential that the BBC hangs on to its core values of accuracy, impartiality, fairness and authority, and adapts them to what audiences want."

In the USA, where multi-channel television is now the norm, rival stations fight tooth and nail for ratings. One of the consequences has been what media commentators call "the dumbing down of news". It involves choosing newscasters for their looks instead of their journalistic skills, going for glamour rather than gravitas, and covering stories with a high shock or schlock quotient.

Chief culprits are the so-called news magazine shows. "The disease of these shows is that breast cancer, wife beating, violence or drugs is going to get the audience's attention rather than foreign policy," explains Howard Stringer, ex-president of CBS, in the final episode of BBC2's *Breaking the News*.

So as British television news faces its biggest expansion for a generation, there is concern that "dumbed down" news programmes, where entertaining viewers takes priority over informing them, may invade our screens and erode standards. Some say it's already started to happen. Cable and satellite channels are already offering different styles of news shows. Live TV's audiences, for example, are treated to a giant rabbit, the so-called News Bunny, who sits behind newsreaders to give a thumbs up or down verdict on the day's stories. Reports of its demise were clearly exaggerated.

"Dumbing down involves reducing the story to what programme-makers believe is the nugget that a certain type of audience wants to see," suggests Chris Cramer, former head of news gathering at BBC TV and now managing editor at Ted Turner's CNN in Atlanta. "There's quite a lot of evidence that dumbing down happens in the States in some measure and to a small degree in the UK."

Triggering much more debate over news dumbing down in Britain was the launch of *Channel 5 News*, presented by eye-catching Kirsty Young.

Rivals are certainly watching its development with keen interest. It is the first new peak-time terrestrial news programme since the birth of *Channel 4 News* in 1982.

At that time, Channel 4's brief was to offer a more in-depth version of the day's events, providing greater reporting of such up-market topics as the arts and business than was customary. It was aimed at an informed, educated audience, the kind of people more likely to read a broadsheet than a tabloid newspaper.

By contrast, Channel 5 is setting out its news stall to appeal to viewers who tend not to watch the news because they think it is "boring" and "not for them". One innovation has been to dispense with the conventional studio desk to lessen the formality. On Channel 5,

Kirsty Young either perches on a piece of furnture in the newsroom, walks around or stands.

Television news veteran Roger Bolton, presenter of Channel 4's *Right to Reply* and former editor of both ITV's *This Week* and BBC1's *Nationwide* (famous for bringing viewers the skateboarding duck), thinks not. "You've got to separate presentation from content," he says. "*Channel 5 News*'s agenda and running order are not significantly different to the other TV news programmes. They're attempting to provide more coverage of popular culture, but they're still leading on the day's main stories."

In fact you could argue that, far from playing to the lowest common denominator, *Channel 5 News* is broadening the range of topics covered by British television news. In recent weeks the programme has devoted a lot of airtime to eco-warriors protesting against an extension of Manchester Airport and ran a lengthy report on a new breed of home-grown cannabis, called "skunk". These stories were treated responsibly, with no sign of the sensationalism that has made American news magazine programmes so controversial. Nor is there the preoccupation with crime, the "if it bleeds, it leads" mentality, that sometimes passed for "news" across the Atlantic.

Press speculation has suggested that the BBC review, designed to discover what audiences want from news programmes, could lead to the end of the dark-suited, middle-aged newscaster. However, *RT*'s recent reader poll showed that Trevor McDonald and Michael Buerk are the two newsreaders viewers trust most.

"All the audience reseach I've seen rates the BBC number one for consistency, accuracy, quality and breadth of coverage," says Richard Ayre, deputy chief executive of BBC News. "Where we sometimes score less well is the friendliness of our approach. For us, the trick is to maintain our commanding authority while also being more approachable and accessible."

And despite concern that news programmes are less popular with the under-35s than they are with older viewers, with a combined total of more than 12 million viewers tuning in to watch the *Nine O'Clock News* on BBC1 and ITN's *News at Ten*, any changes designed to meet the challenges of the new digital millennium, when more than 200 channels may be available in every home, are likely to be gradual.

"I am very optimistic about the future of TV news," says Richard Tait, ITN's editor-in-chief. "Far from dumbing down I think we've smartened up in recent years. The days when actors read the news have gone for ever. Audiences are intelligent and expect news to carry weight. I think the best is yet to come." *RT*

COMMENTARY

The term 'dumbing down' is a fairly recent entry into debates about the media. Conventionally the word 'dumb' has been used in British English to mean 'unable to speak'. In American English it has long meant 'stupid' as in 'dumb blonde'. Its current use on both sides of the Atlantic as a verb idiom, 'to dumb down', reflects a well known process whereby words shift from traditional noun and adjectival function and become verbs. Similar examples are:

- parent→parenting
- bottle→to bottle out
- access (noun)→access (verb)
- fast-track→as in 'We shall fast-track your application'.

The shift in meaning is from being a thing or a quality to doing an action. In the case of 'dumbing down' it is ironic that while its intended meaning is 'to make things simple for our customers' it carries with it the unintended older meaning of being unable to speak at all.

In 1997, the BBC showed a series of programmes called *Breaking The News*, which discussed how American news magazine programmes found that sex and violence boosted ratings, while equivalent Russian programmes found that disasters had the same effect. Steve Clark investigated TV news in the UK to see whether or not news was being presented in ways that would be more entertaining, thereby boosting ratings.

The caption to Steve Clark's article contains the words 'revealed' and 'investigates', conveying the sense of a plot or at least something that doesn't want to be enquired into too closely. Notice too the oppositions set up: glamour versus gravitas; entertaining versus informing; sense of responsibility versus sensationalism.

Tim Gardam's comment about audiences is interesting: 'They regard it [TV News] as a closed language with insiders talking to each other.'

ACTIVITY 29

. . . and dumber

The following text, 'Television Hits The Dumber Switch', by Ferdinand Mount, appeared in *The Sunday Times* (2 February, 1998). Read it and answer the following questions:

1 What role is assigned to the reader? How are you expected to respond?
2 What is the implied outlook or world view of the author?
3 How does the writer use language to elicit the reader's response? Look, for example, at the opening anecdote. Why has it been used? Look also at the beginning of the last paragraph, 'My real complaint . . .'. What then is the purpose of the preceding paragraphs?

TEXT 24

No respectable person actually admits to dumbing down. The thing to do before commencing operation is to spray a cloud of verbiage about "modernisation" and "communication", so as to put people off the scent. Last week I read a whole article written by Sir Peter North, principal of Jesus College, Oxford, about his plans for modernising the university. At the end of it I still didn't have a clue what he was up to. I found out elsewhere that he wants to make the final exams less daunting and rely more on continuous assessment.

"Fluffy-headed females can't be expected to cope with the demands, so it must all be made a little easier for them. Can you imagine anything more preposterous and patronising? Well, yes, I can, in fact. What you do is to take half a dozen television producers and ask them to give their views on almost anything you fancy – the arts, religion, education, the monarchy.

Last week the subject was politics. Mr Tony Hall, who rejoices in one of those glorious BBC titles, chief executive of news and current affairs, told a gathering of Labour, Conservative and Liberal Democrat spokesmen that the BBC intended to reduce the number of television and radio interviews with politicians, because the public found them so boring. The previous week all the television networks joined together to announce plans to reduce the number of party political broadcasts as well, and preferably restrict them to election time, because the viewers always switch them off and can't really understand them.

BBC research has, we are told, revealed that even in the ABC1 groups half the public don't know what a backbencher or a select committee is.

Observe carefully here the brilliant use of the dumber-down's double-barrelled technique. On the one hand, politicians are all pompous old bores, hopelessly out of touch and unable to express themselves in plain English. On the other hand, the viewers are a bunch of ignorant twerps, with the attention span of a mosquito. Which leaves only the television producer – sharp-witted, supremely cool, with designer jacket and dazzling lifestyle – to condescend to entertain us with material that our pea brains might conceivably encompass.

This godlike creature planes like an eagle above the surface of the planet – in business class, of course – bringing back gobbets of human life to our humdrum nests.

It never, of course, occurs to television producers or presenters that the shortcomings of politics on the box might be anything to do with them. If I were to suggest that television interviewers are often not only rude (which I don't mind, nor do most politicians, as politics is a rough trade), but also conceited, underbriefed and woefully deficient in historical grasp or intellectual curiosity, I would be drummed out of the BBC canteen.

Meanwhile, the telly plods on down towards the bottom end of the market without a backwards glance. There is at present not a single television programme on books. And the most intellectually demanding programme is probably A Question of Sport. I last saw a good new play on television at some period in the later Stone Age. The vein of genius that used now and then to infuse the British sitcom seems to have dried up.

Even before we lost the great Frank Muir, the BBC had decided his memoirs were "too literary" for Radio 4. As for documentaries, even the ITV companies are now attacking Channel 4 for its "drift to populism". And the Campaign for Quality Television is simultaneously attacking ITV for sowing its serious documentaries so thinly and randomly that they have become virtually invisible. In any case, what most documentaries tell you nowadays are amazing things such as that smoking is bad for you and that prostitutes work for money.

We naturally think of television as being the most modern force in society, and the medium still attracts its share of the liveliest young recruits, but in a curious way it has become ossified and hopelessly conventional, much more so than institutions notorious for being stuffy, such as the bar and the Jockey Club.

My real complaint is not about the lack of talent on display. Talent is an unpredictable commodity that cannot be whistled up to order. What is more serious is the absence of aspiration in high places, and the contentment with the tatty and trivial. For that we must blame, not the creative spirits, but the suits who stifle them.

COMMENTARY

In this article Mount appears to regard insults as a form of entertainment, and TV as a legitimate target. Possibly we are seeing here an inevitable rivalry between two big media powers, newspapers and TV. Notice at least two consumer references: 'bottom end of the market' and 'talent is an unpredictable commodity'.

The article sets up an opposition between a 'drift to populism' and the *Campaign for Quality TV.* What do you think 'populism' is? Check the word in a dictionary. In his article, Steve Clarke uses the phrase 'popular culture'. The two terms are not interchangeable. 'Populism' is a determination to win over the largest number of people (as in audience ratings) by appealing to what Clarke calls, 'the lowest common denominator'. 'Popular culture' on the other hand includes all those things that large numbers of people share and enjoy; sport, music, seaside holidays, fairgrounds, hobbies, discos, food, comedians.

What do you think would typify populism and quality for Ferdinand Mount? What typifies them for you? Give an example of quality writing and populist writing.

Notice, finally, Mount ends with the phrase, 'television ... the most modern force in society', reminding us again of a power we take for granted.

ACTIVITY 30

The XXX Files

The text below is an abridged version of a long review in the *Independent* by Ian Parker. He is actually reviewing two programmes but his article has become a polemic against a trend in TV documentaries. Summarise the criticisms in your own words. Where does Parker resort to humour, an inherently subversive way of using language, and how would you describe his humour?

TEXT 25

Seeming is believing

By Ian Parker

Faced with an ordinary phenomenon, popular factual televison likes to speak of it as a mystery. The uninteresting or fradulent or coincidental becomes 'weird' – in *Fortean TV*, in *Louis Theroux's Weird Weekends*, in show after show featuring alien abductions and Uri Geller and Carol Vorderman. And in a similar but reverse tradition, modern TV programmes about complex things like to suggest that they have drawn all complexity from their subjects. So the 'truth about women' is somehow lodged in an interview with Zoë Ball; or a little biographical film will strut around as a 'secret life'. We lose out each way. The things that need explaining are not explained, and the things that need no explanation – or only the simplest explanation – become **The Unexplained** (Sky 1).

The Unexplained does battle each week with common sense; it makes every effort not to lose its grip on stupidity. Last week, a Mexican presidential candidate was said to have predicted his own assassination; a photograph was produced of someone who at the time it was taken was meant to be dead; a Hollywood star was visited by a ghost. A whispering, cigar-smoking narrator talked of 'a modest pile of ashes' at the scene of alleged spontaneous combustion (the scene was reconstructed: a modest pile of ashes, and a modest pair of feet coming out of the ashes).

Best of all, we heard how a woman in New Mexico ran over her son's dog. (Another reconstruction: slight bump in the road – front wheels – then another slight bump.) The son was very upset. Brownie, the dog, was buried. But the next day, Brownie appeared on the front porch, alive if not unscathed. (His eye had popped out, which the family thought 'cute', since it gave the impression the dog was winking.) The man of the house was interviewed in a big hat, and he explained how this supernatural event had utterly changed his life: nothing would ever be the same again. And then he added, as an aside, 'but we're not getting rich or anything like that'. You could see his disappointment: to have brought such a perfect dish to TV's table – dog, small boy, low key violence, life after death – and not profited. This, indeed, was hard to explain.

The Unexplained tries to concoct modern magic out of nothing, but its Tuesday-night companion on Sky was heading, unexpectedly, in the oppsiite direction. **Breaking The Magician's Code: Magic's Biggest Secrets Finally Revealed** was the rarest of things – an American TV documentary able to keep, with honour, its promise of complete demystification. In the field of destroying the simple pleasures of children, television can sometimes be fearlessly rigorous.

Everyone loves a spoilsport: with many flourishes, a magician – masked for the sake of anonymity – did his tricks, and then he did them again in a manner that gave away the illusion. The rabbit, it turned out, was hooked under the table in a black handkerchief. The woman was not levitating, but was being held in the air by a forklift truck parked behind the curtain. Subsequently, she was not sawn in half, but had curled herself into one half of the box (when you see feet wriggling at the end, they are, apparently, artificial and remote controlled). The elephant had not disappeared in a puff of smoke – it was standing behind mirrors, looking tired.

Shop Till You Drop (C4) claimed to be from the same TV stable as *Magic's Biggest Secrets*. It was going to show how we 'fall prey' to retail trickery. This is a subject much loved by magazine features writers and TV documentary makers: we seem to have heard many times how supermarkets blow the scent of baking bread into the faces of passing customers; and how they aim, where possible, to have us travel in a clockwise direction through supermarkets, starting with aubergines. This series, however, is interested in fashion shopping, and it therefore seems to have put itself at a disadvantage – given that so much of the business of selling clothes happens outside the shop, in magazines and in pop videos and in people's heads.

In last week's first part, it was hard to see the evidence of trickery. We heard how 'a small army' of marketing experts – in a manner said to be fiendish and sophisticated – had divided fashion into four categories. These were The Fashion Enthusiasts (meaning young); The Interested Label-Seekers (rich); The Price-Led Replacers (poor) and the Thirtysomethings (people in their thirties).

The experts had clever beards and worked in the fields of design, consumer psychology and staff training. They contemplated video footage of shoppers and entered information into electronic organisers, perhaps details of their fees. This was not a good advertisement for their various alleged sciences. It seemed that where they were not being foolish they were stating the obvious. But the thought crossed one's mind: perhaps the experts are designed to look foolish; perhaps their primary purpose is to speak unconvincingly on television, and so protect their masters from harsher judgments.

Looking forward, watching this week's second part of *Shop Till You Drop,* it was hard not to notice that it is almost exactly the same as last week's: the same footage of the same shoppers, many of the same phrases used by the narrator. Here, at last, is the evidence: here is retail trickery at its most audacious and fascinating. Channel 4 has bought a six-part series made out of six identical programmes.

COMMENTARY

In *Seeming is Believing* interesting and conflicting motivations are identified. First there is the desire of the TV company to entertain by informing, a genre sometimes referred to as 'infotainment'. But at the same time it wishes to mystify us with *The Unexplained*, which has echoes of the genuinely fictional *The X-Files*. Secondly there is the mixture of exposure journalism (tricks of customer manipulation) and what Parker calls 'proxy shopping'. Parker's own motivation appears to be to cast serious doubt on the value of both kinds of programmes. His argument is lucid and his humour scathing at two particular points:

- 'WE lose out each way'
- 'The things that need explaining are not explained, and the things that need no explanation – or only the simplest explanation – become THE UNEXPLAINED'
- 'There is retail trickery at its most audacious and fascinating. Channel Four has bought a six-part series made out of six identical programmes.'

ACTIVITY 31

Political slanging

Below is an article from the *Guardian* (2 July 1998). It reports a dispute between two powerful influences on public opinion, the BBC and the government itself. Read the article, making a note of emotive words and phrases. Be absolutely clear who says what about whom and which is the voice of the writer. In the headline, for instance, 'trivial' is a quotation whereas the voice of the newspaper comes through in the choice of the word 'flays'.

TEXT 26

Spin doctors furious over coverage of maverick's swipe at Blair, women MPs and millennium dome

Labour flays 'trivial' BBC

Kamal Ahmed and Anne Perkins

THE BBC's relationship with the Government took a fresh nosedive yesterday when the Labour Party described Radio 4's World at One programme as trivial and lacking perspective.

In a terse statement, a spokesman said that the programme's coverage of a speech by the Labour MP Brian Sedgemore, in which the veteran backbencher attacked Tony Blair as "above God" and Labour's women MPs as "Stepford wives", was typical of a corporation driven by news editors who simply wanted to attack the Government.

The World at One devoted 13 minutes of its 40-minute programme to Mr Sedgemore's speech at the Tate Gallery in London, which was circulated to political correspondents on Thursday night to make sure it would not be missed.

As well as attacking the Prime Minister, Mr Sedgemore, a maverick who was one of the 47 Labour MPs who voted against the cut in benefits for lone parents, also turned his fire on Peter Mandelson, the Minister Without Portfolio.

He described the Millennium Dome as "Mandy's Folly, which at a staggering cost of £850 million will give the country the Secret Policeman's politically correct vision of the future."

He said some women Labour MPs had computer chips inserted in their brains to keep them "on message".

A Labour Party spokesman described the speech as a silly stunt from a man who was "permamently out of line with the party".

A later statement then took up the attack on the BBC's coverage.

"For the BBC to think that this is the most important thing to happen today and devote 13 minutes of radio time to it demonstrates their complete loss of perspective and their increasingly trivial agendas which we have come to expect," an official said.

The latest row comes after a series of public battles between the Government and the BBC.

On Wednesday Alastair Campbell, the Prime Minister's press secretary, rebuked one of the corporation's most senior political staff for raising the issue of Monica Lewinsky during Mr Blair's visit to America.

John Sergeant, the BBC's chief political correspondent, asked Mr Campbell if Mr Blair was worried that he might be questioned about the sexual scandal surrounding the American President, Bill Clinton.

Mr Campbell dismissed Mr Sergeant's question as "irrelevant" and attacked the BBC as a "downmarket, dumbed-down, over-staffed, over bureaucratic, ridiculous organisation".

Last month Mr Campbell and Gregor McKay, William Hague's spokesman, criticised BBC news at a seminar organised by the corporation's chief executive of news, Tony Hall.

In December the Labour Party threatened to suspend co-operation with the BBC after John Humphrys, a presenter of the Today programme, clashed with Harriet Harman, the social security secretary, on air.

"Why don't they concentrate on the bigger issues?" a government source asked.

The BBC hit back at its critics, saying that it was its job to scrutinise government policy.

"They are ridiculous," a senior news executive said. "They want to control what we do. Mr Sedgemore's speech was not made in a vacuum and many others are sympathetic to what Mr Sedgemore was saying."

"The Labour Party put up Gerald Kaufman, who gave a vigorous defence of the party for 3½ minutes. It was perfectly balanced."

• Sir Julian Critchley the rebel Tory who retired at the last election renewed his attack on the party yesterday, describing it as "anti-black and unattractive".

Sir Julian, former MP for Aldershot and biographer of Michael Heseltine, told The Oldie magazine that he preferrred Tony Blair to William Hague.

He said: "The Tory party shows every sign of becoming a right-wing rump, obscurantist and nationalist. They are certainly anti-black. By and large, most of them are so unattractive I wonder that I stayed with them as long as I did."

He praised Tony Blair: "He has dragged the Labour Party kicking and screaming into the last part of the 20th century . . . and that is no mean achievement."

A Conservative Central Office spokesman said last night: "Sir Julian is sometimes entertaining but never enlightening. I'm surprised that anyone takes anything he says seriously."

COMMENTARY

Notice the words chosen by the *Guardian* in the superscript: spin doctors, maverick, swipe.

Frequently the people quoted are placed in adversarial roles (in conflict with each other). So called 'quality broadsheets' are usually differentiated from tabloids as being less sensationalist. There is, however, a strong semantic field in the article that can hardly be called polite: furious, swipe, nose-dive, above God, attack (twice), maverick, staggering, inserted in their brains, public battles, silly stunt, row, sexual scandal, ridiculous, clashed, anti-black, kicking and screaming.

ACTIVITY 32

Cool Britannia

The following text was written by John Harlow for *The Sunday Times* (8 February, 1998). The Arts Council of Great Britain is funded by the government to support The Arts. Harlow's article draws attention to an apparent change in policy.

Read the article noting all the words and phrases used to describe any kind of cultural activity. What contrasts are drawn? Write a letter to the editor explaining your priorities for the limited budget available to subsidise 'The Arts'.

TEXT 27

Arts Council sidelines ballet to bolster 'cool Britannia'

by John Harlow
Arts Correspondent

THE ARTS Council, Britain's most stubborn defender of "high culture", is embracing "cool Britannia". Opera and ballet are to be pushed aside in favour of fashion and popular music in the most radical shake-up in the arts system since the second world war.

The blueprint for change will be presented to the council's ruling body this week in an attempt to stave off even more far-reaching proposals under consideration by Chris Smith, the culture secretary. Options incude abolishing the council.

The reforms reflect the passions of Tony Blair, the former rock guitarist who has excelled in creating photo opportunities by inviting such showbusiness personalities as Noel Gallagher, of Oasis, to Downing Street while not finding time for "old arts" such as theatre.

Blair has ensured that his government's policies are wrapped in the flag of British artistic success, even labelling his reforms of state benefits as "the full monty".

However, such manoeuvrings are increasingly being rejected by the "cool Britannia" icons themselves. Last week Wayne Hemmingway, founder of the Red or Dead fashion house, said that intertwining of the Establishment with popular culture was neither clever nor funny. "I do not think the Arts Council will be any more successful at this than the politicians," he said.

The Arts Council's self-defence plan includes amending its royal charter so that it can seek out hitherto-scorned areas of popular culture for backing. It would give money to underground pop music clubs, fringe art galleries and anti-Establishment publishing venues in the hope that they mature into lucrative mainstream art forms.

Insiders say that pop groups such as Prodigy, who burst out of clubland, or controversial designers such as Alexander McQueen and John Galliano, would have been eligible for Arts Council grants under the proposed new emphasis.

Individual grants to budding McQueens for materials or instruments will be tiny compared with the millons that go into the Royal Opera House, but there will be thousands of applicants.

The switch will provoke charges of "dumbing down", but council members, exasperated by the antics of the guardians of high culture at the Royal Opera House and elsewhere, will claim that they may have had an unfair slice of the cake for too long.

Christopher Frayling, rector of the Royal College of Art admitted the changes might smack of opportunism: "It may sound all too cool Britannia and trendy but this is where the next generation of our cultural industry talent is coming from."

Francis Maude, Conservative culture spokesman, warned that Arts Council interest could mean the beginning of the end for cool Britannia. "I would warn any young artist to stay away from the clammy embrace of public subsidy," he said. "It comes with too many strings."

Others fear that scholarships to help buy electric guitars might stifle the rebellious spirit of young artists. Hirst himself has said that art is the ultimate form of free enterprise, as well as free expression.

COMMENTARY Note the opposition between film and pop music and the 'older arts'. Note also the implied generation gap in the use of 'older'. Note too the connection made between culture and consumerism in the idea of art as 'free enterprise', and the notion of 'cultural industry talent'. The phrase 'seedcorn grant' recalls the much older, agricultural meaning of the word 'culture' as in cultivating growth from seed. What do you think the slogan Cool Britannia means? Who is promoting it? What are the economic advantages?

ACTIVITY 33

Let's have a party

The text below is a notice that was pinned up by the party organiser in a prestigious 'executive residence' (name withheld). It is reproduced from an essay by Michael Halliday in *Literacy and Society* edited by Hasan and Williams (Longman, 1996).

Read the notice and answer the following questions:

1 What role does it assign to the reader? How do you react?
2 What is taken for granted about lifestyle? What underlying world view is there?
3 What are the details of lexis and grammar that enable you to answer 1 and 2?

TEXT 28

Dear tenant
IF YOU JUST WANNA HAVE FUN . . .
Come to *your* MOONCAKE NITE THEME PARTY next Saturday.
That's September 20 – from 7.30 p.m. until the wee hours!!
A sneak preview of the exciting line-up of activities incudes:

* Mr/Ms   Tenant Contest
* Find *Your* Mooncake Partner
* Pass the Lantern Game
* Bottoms Up Contest
* Blow the Lantern Game
* Moonwalking Contest
* DANCING
* PLUS MORE! MORE! MORE!

For even greater fun, design and wear your original Mooncake creation, and bring our self-made lantern passport!
But don't despair if you can't because this party is *FOR* you!
Lantern passports can be bought at the door.
Just c'mon and grab this opportunity to chat up your neighbour.
Call yours truly on *ext. 137* NOW! Confirm you really wanna have fun!! Why – September 20's next Saturday.
See you!

Public Relations Officer
P.S. Bring your camera to 'capture' the fun!

COMMENTARY

The chapter ends with Halliday's own commentary on this text, which demonstrates that linguists can be polemical as well as analytical. Text 29 is not an easy read but it does demonstrate very well the way in which ideology can be discovered through discourse analysis.

Some of Halliday's terms are explained first:

- *lexico-grammar* – simply refers to the combined workings of the lexical and grammatical choices of the writer
- *semiotically* – semiotics are the signs or clues a reader can notice by which a writer presents himself knowingly or unknowingly (clothes can be read as semiotics telling something about the wearer)
- *literacy* – not just being able to read and write but the consequences of living in a literate culture.

What do you think Halliday means by his invented term 'disneyfication'? It is certainly a scathing comment. Refer back to the earlier text on Mickey Mouse culture.

TEXT 29

In the cacophony of voices that constitute this text, we can recognise a number of oppositions: child and adult, work and leisure, 'naughty' and 'nice', professional and commercial – constructed by the lexicogrammar in cahoots with the prosody and paralanguage. But this mixture of bureaucratic routine, comics-style graphic effects, masculine aggression, childism and condescension, straight commercialism, conspiratorialism and hype adds up to something that we recognize: late capitalist English in the Disneyland register. Presumably there are institutions in southern California where people who are being trained to 'service' business executives to learn to construct this kind of discourse. The context is the disneyfication of western man (I say 'man' advisedly), whereby the off-duty executive reverts semiotically to childhood while retaining the material make-up of an adult.

Literacy today includes many contexts of this contorted kind, where the functions of the written text have to be sorted out at various levels.

Summary

In this chapter you have explored the idea of culture because language is inseparably bound up with cultural values and beliefs. A better understanding of how language is used can be achieved by an appreciation of the culture to which a text belongs.

Particular aspects of modern culture, such as communications media, consumerism and entertainment were explored in mainly polemical texts arguing about the quality and value of these influences on our lives.

Particular issues raised that are directly relevant to how language is used were:

- the power of news editors
- the claimed 'dumbing down' of news programmes
- the claimed conversion of information into entertainment
- the effects of the use of metaphors derived from economics (eg commodities, consumers, enterprise, market) to describe the arts and other cultural activities.

The chapter concluded with a demonstration by Michael Halliday of how cultural values and ideology generate particular styles of discourse that in their choice of language, signal those values explicitly and implicitly.

4 Reel Women: Language, Power and Gender

In this chapter you are going to investigate texts that raise questions about perceived changes in gender roles at work, in advertising and the media and in pop culture.

Texts are grouped in the following sequence:

- women in the office and the armed services
- students and women MPs
- images of beauty and desire
- women and cars
- the Spice Girls' manifesto.

You will have opportunities to develop further your skill in stylistics, especially in relating words and images, and to extend your understanding of discourse, social power and the ideologies that connect the two.

Gender issues

The overall perspective for this book is language and society. So far you have considered the following aspects of language:

- discourse
- lexico-grammatical choices
- text construction.

You have also considered the following aspects of modern society:

- culture/lifestyle
- consumerism
- communications media.

Stylistics and discourse analysis will help you to see the connections between these six things and should make the phrase 'language and society' seem less vague. This will save you from pointless feature spotting.

All six of the above strands come together when exploring gender issues. But don't try to explore them all at once. Always be sure which connection you are making at any one time, for example, lexical choices in a text describing new style office secretaries. Sometimes the strands come together of their own accord as you work through a text, but there is always an opportunity to pull ideas together at the end of your investigation.

Issues of language deserve a book of their own to describe the changes in ideas and attitudes between the 1960s and the 1990s. If you are interested in feminist ideas about language you should read:

- *Talking Power: The Politics of Language*, by Robin Lakoff (1990)
- *The Feminist Critique of Language*, edited by Deborah Cameron (1990)
- *Women, Men and Language*, by Jennifer Coates (1993)
- *The New Pygmalion: Verbal Hygiene for Women*, a chapter in Deborah Cameron's *Verbal Hygiene* (1995).

Let's begin with an excerpt from the last of these books. By 'verbal hygiene', Deborah Cameron means 'the urge to meddle in matters of language'. This isn't entirely a joke for she goes on to say that once we start reflecting on how language is being used, we start to notice that there is more to it than just the words; that behind it we can find manipulation, ambiguity, sloppy thinking and so on. If this sounds to you a bit like stylistics or discourse analysis, you would not be far wrong.

ACTIVITY 34

From rags to riches

Read the following excerpt and summarise Cameron's argument. Then write your own view under the title: 'Language and Love'. If you wish, you could also read the first chapter of Deborah Tannen's best seller, *You Just Don't Understand* (1990).

TEXT 30

FROM RAGS TO RICHES: LANGUAGE, GENDER AND TRANSFORMATION

In his preface to *Pygmalion*, one of the great verbal hygiene stories of modern English literature, George Bernard Shaw remarked: 'it is impossible for an Englishman to open his mouth without making some other Englishman despise him.' To illustrate his thesis, however, Shaw created not an Englishman but an English*woman*, the cockney flower-seller Eliza Doolittle. Eliza plays Galatea to Henry Higgins's Pygmalion: Higgins, a skilled phonetician, makes a bet that he can take the dustman's daughter and in a few months pass her off in London society as a duchess. Higgins, we learn, is a professional specialist in this kind of verbal hygiene. At the beginning of the play he is asked: 'But is there a living in that?' He replies: 'Oh yes. Quite a fat one. This is an age of upstarts' (Shaw 1972: 679).

Pygmalion is conventionally read as a play about class, but it is also quite strikingly a play about gender. It cannot be an accident that Shaw made his working-class 'upstart' a woman, for *Pygmalion* – the title alludes to the classical myth of the creator who falls in love with his own creation – belongs to a narrative genre with certain assumptions about gender built into it. It seems 'natural' (in other words, culturally predictable) that the powerful creator should be male and the malleable creature female, and also that the class hierarchy between the two should reinforce rather than contradict the gender hierarchy. Nor will it surprise us if the story turns into a romance, with creator and created finally confessing mutual adoration and falling into each other's arms – a clichéd ending, but one that a great deal of our reading, from childhood fairy-tales onwards, has led us to expect and desire.

Shaw himself took some pains to thwart conventional expectations. The text of his play ends not with a love scene between Eliza and Higgins, but with a note spelling out that Eliza marries the younger, poorer and less powerful Freddy; a note which begins:

> The rest of the story . . . would hardly need telling if our imaginations were not so enfeebled by their lazy dependence on the ready-mades and reach-me-downs of the rag-shop where Romance keeps its stock of 'happy endings' to misfit all stories.

Shaw was clear that for Eliza, marrying Higgins would not be a happy ending . . .

But later adaptors and audiences thought otherwise. Both the film *Pygmalion* and the musical *My Fair Lady* were given the romantic treatment Shaw had rejected. That this change was deemed necessary when the stage play was adapted for more popular media might seem to confirm that many people's imaginations are dependent on the ready-made formulas of fairy-tales and romance. Yet it is notable that Shaw's own imagination could conceive of only one ending to the story of a woman 'upstart': marriage. He spared Eliza the tyrannical Higgins and gave her the ineffectual Freddy, but the logic of his narrative impelled him to marry her to somebody. In fiction, when women successfully transform themselves, whether physically, morally or, as in Eliza's case linguistically, the love of an eligible man is their traditional reward.

The conventions of fiction in this instance are rooted in the conventions of reality. Why are there so many stories in which a powerful man remakes a woman in the image he desires and then possesses her – or alternatively, hands her to another man – and so few where the gender roles are reversed? Presumably it has something to do with the fact that for many groups of women in many historical periods, male approval has been the best guarantee, if not the only one, of economic security and social respectability. Such women have had good reason to try and become what men wanted women to be: they have had a powerful incentive to practise self-improvement. If one consequence of their situation has been the popularity of fictions based on the rags-to-riches formula, another, more practical result has been a lengthy tradition of advice literature specifically addressed to women and dealing with all aspects of their duties, appearance and behaviour. In this corpus of literature the question of women's speech has occupied a not insignificant place.

Although advice for women on speaking is not a recent invention, both its content and the forms in which it circulates have altered over time. Today's version of Eliza Doolittle is defined primarily by her gender rather than her class. It is not her accent but her entire linguistic persona that needs remodelling, and all kinds of verbal hygiene practices have sprung up to assist her in this task. If she is especially privileged or publicly visible she may seek the advice of an image consultant; otherwise she may take a course, or join a group, or sample one of the many advice books on the market. For women of slender means, similar advice is offered in women's magazines and on daytime television.

ACTIVITY 35

Back at the office

In Chapter One you looked at an office conversation (Sid and Rita) taken from another book by Tannen. Look now at the following article by the managing director of an office staff recruitment bureau. Summarise its argument first. Next, decide what role it assigns to you, the reader? What does it assume about you? Then describe what you think is the ideology, the value system, the outlook behind the text. Finally, note carefully just what are the features of language on which you base your judgements.

TEXT 31

Why Secretary is not A DIRTY WORD

By Richard Grace, MD of Gordon Yates and a member of the Secretarial Advertising Forum

It's fascinating, isn't it, how words can depreciate in value, just like money.

A pound in Shakespeare's day was worth very many times what a pound is worth today. Inflation has depreciated its value steadily over the years.

So too some of the words Shakespeare used. "I'll be with you presently" meant, then, "I'll be with you immediately". These days, of course, "presently" means the same as "in due course" or "in a while".

None of us really like to be rushed, do we? And so over the centuries, the meaning of the word has changed to suit our preference better.

It's the same with the word "secretary".

During the last century, a "secretary" was quite rare and extremely important. Occupying a key position of power and influence, he (yes, he was almost certainly male!) held all the "secrets" – taking care of all the administrative affairs of, perhaps, a major landowner, or a general, or a bishop.

During the present century, this situation has gradually changed. As businesses began to expand, helped by Henry Ford's techniques for mass production and the growth of all kinds of great industries, so grew the ranks of business administrators – all kinds of managers, great and small – all with their own offices and (by now, very often female) secretaries.

Fifty years ago, when Gordon Yates was just starting out as a "secretarial recruitment bureau", there was a pretty clear divide between "typists" and "secretaries". The "typists" did typing while the "secretaries" did diaries, shorthand, organised meetings, travel, that sort of thing.

In the meantime, the traditional "secretaries" (ie,

those working for bishops and the like) began to separate themselves from this new, office-based breed by calling themselves "personal assistants".

And so to the steady depreciation of job titles of the last 30–40 years – a period during which "typists" have sought to be called "secretaries", "secretaries" have sought to be called "personal assistants" and "personal assistants" have begun to seek refuge in titles such as "executive assistant".

Which leaves us where?

On the one hand, we have serious professional bodies such as IQPS (the Institute of Qualified Professional Secretaries) and EAPS (the European Association of Professional Secretaries) working assiduously to enhance and promote the "secretary" as a highly professional role.

On the other hand, we have (unenlightened?) people registering with Gordon Yates and other recruitment companies, who come in looking for work that's "a bit less secretarial" – in other words, they're looking for something with a bit less typing. Such people, perhaps, aspire to "P.A." work. But these days, it's by no means rare for a so-called "PA" or "Personal Assistant" – to be working for a *team* of people! And *still* doing typing for a fair old chunk of the day!

We need to come back to Shakespeare, and to that famous quote: "a rose by any other name" still smells as sweet. What, in truth, is there in a name?

Whether a person doing a job is called a "typist", a "secretary", a "PA", an "Executive Assistant" or even a "large turnip" surely matters not a jot. What matters is whether the job is worth doing (in which case it's worth doing well) and whether the person doing it has the skills needed in order to do it well.

Like so much else in life today, support staff roles are changing rapidly. In some leading-edge companies (Microsoft is just one example), "secretary" as a job title has already been killed off. This doesn't mean that they don't have any use for "secretaries". But it does mean that companies are looking at role content more than role titles. They're placing more emphasis on graphics skills. They want pro-active, customer-focused team players. They need skilled office professionals, able to turn the latest emerging technologies into business advantage. And so far, whatever the role title, it has in fact very much been the "secretary" who has tended to ride this wave and stay at the forefront of change.

If the "secretary" keeps "secrets" these days, it is likely to be those to do with IT software – advanced Powerpoint, Word macros, Internet/Intranet, all that kind of stuff. Information is power. In a world increasingly ruled by computers, those who command the software command real power.

And yet, a warning note needs to be sounded.

So far, we have all been communicating with our computers via the keyboard. This has given "secretaries" a unique advantage: they have been able to communicate faster than anyone else. Accordingly, they have tended very quickly to put themselves ahead of the game through all of the incredible changes and upgrades in PC power which we have experienced during the last 15 or so years.

But watch out! Voice-activated computers are already with us and will almost certainly render keyboards obsolete within the next five years. At long last, the "secretary" will break free from the tyranny of typing – but at the cost of what has been a pretty important strategic "secretarial" advantage to date.

When this happens the best "secretaries" will do what they've always done, and add value in a hundred different ways totally unconnected with the keyboard.

It's going to be an invigorating new world, but strictly for those who are ready and able to take advantage.

COMMENTARY

The title of the article is an interesting one which raises the question, 'for whom?' women employees? men? To whom is the article addressed? Note that it sets up the article as an argument against a perceived point of view.

Look at the style of the opening and closing sentences. These always contain strong discourse signals, especially in a tight word limit. Both are confidently declarative, though the first contains a tag question that draws the reader in. The last three paragraphs introduce a new theme and a new technological ideology. Is it a warning? A threat?

Notice the use of the word 'those'. Who are they assumed to be? Are you one of them? Do you think the role assigned here is progressive-minded, potential employee? Or is it offering an explanation of why you might be out of work in the near future?

The origin of this text is unusual. Normally, in books and examinations, as much relevant information as possible is given about the origin of a text, but working on the text first and then placing it in its practical context, emphasises that it is social context that shapes language into discourse. The text comes from a free, weekly magazine called *London Alive In 9 to 5* (Issue 780, 23 June, 1997). It was handed to one of the authors while he was walking across London Bridge to a management conference. The magazine is published by Independent Magazines UK Ltd and its pages are almost entirely devoted to job advertisements and to advertisements by employment agencies. There was a little bit of gossip about media stars at the beginning in addition to Richard Grace's article.

ACTIVITY 36

Women go to war

The texts below were taken from *The Times* (7 February, 1998). The first is a news report, the second an excerpt from an analysis of the news on the editorial page.

A quite significant social change is being reported here involving one of the armed forces (note the word 'force' here).

Having read the news item, look at the editorial. What do you observe about the arguments and attitudes in it? Take particular note of words such as 'hazing', 'unreconstructed', 'potential war zone'.

Comment too on the British forces' reluctance to allow women to be interviewed. What sort of power do interviews confer that there could be this reluctance?

TEXT 32a

Women to command warships

THE Royal Navy has ended centuries of tradition by appointing two women to command warships, it emerged yesterday. Susan Moore and Melanie Rees, both 26-year-old lieutenants, are embarking on a special course next week and should take up their posts within weeks.

The appointment of the two women – who will begin by commanding Archer class coastal patrol boats with a crew of five – follows a series of scandals on board ships related to mixed crews.

The latest move, however, has been welcomed by MPs and the Equal Opportunities Commission. Karmlesh Bahl, the commission's chairwoman, said: "These appointments send a great message to all young people with aspirations to join the Armed Forces." Dr John Reid, the Armed Forces Minister, said: "Appointments such as these clearly demonstrate the Royal Navy's commitment to full integration of women."

Lt Moore will take command of *HMS Dasher* at Portsmouth and Lt Rees will command *HMS Exeter*, based at Cardiff.

TEXT 32b

Less dangerous, but also a big headline-grabber, is the question of sexual relations within the forces, from harassment to adultery. *HMS Brilliant* produced a crew pregnancy and an adulterous liaison on its first trial with women seven years ago; there have been half a dozen sexual harassment cases since the forces became more mixed in the 1990s, and internal reports as late as 1994, in the case of the Navy, showed that men were "unreconstructed" in their attitudes.

In America, whole military bases have been investigated for "hazing" – vicious initiation rites – which were particularly cruel to women, and dozens of senior men have been discharged for harassment. Then there was the case of Lt Kelly Flynn, the first female B52 bomber pilot, who was given a "general" discharge after an affair with a married colleague.

Initial suggestions, by those who wished to keep the forces segregated, that cameraderie would fall apart with the entry of women seem to be largely unfounded. People behave much as they do working in civilian offices.

In some ways, the British forces' reluctance to allow women to be interviewed in a potential war zone is understandable. The first women to qualify as fighter pilots were fêted by the media, to their own embarrassment and the annoyance of their male colleagues. Flt Lt Melanie Rolfe, speaking for the RAF, said: "There were teething problems created by constantly drawing attention to female aircrew, who just wanted to do the same job as men – quietly."

That said, if the role models are kept under wraps, they will be of little use in recruitment, and the British forces, with a shortfall of 5,000 staff, are relying increasingly on women. Women make up 13 per cent of the three forces, compared with half that seven years ago. The RAF press office pointed out the usefulness of women: "More than physical size, you need intelligence to cope with the myriad inputs when you're flying at 600 knots at night. It's hard enough just avoiding flying into a hill, never mind dropping a bomb."

However, the combat debate is by no means over, at least for the British Army, which still bans women from the tank corps and infantry. "We're keeping it under review," a spokesman said.

The Army spokesman said it was really a question of whether British society as a whole was ready to see women at the sharp end of combat. "How will the public react to limbless ex-servicewomen in The Mall on Remembrance Sunday?" he said.

In Chapter Three you looked at a report of a political slanging match between the government and the BBC. Underneath it lay a very serious concern of the government that the BBC influenced opinion far more effectively than the government. The text below, from the *Daily Telegraph* (7 February, 1998), focuses on remarks made about labour women MPs.

ACTIVITY 37

Summarise what is said and note especially the kinds of language used. This text is made up of a number of voices. Make clear which are the views of Jon Hibbs, explicitly and implicitly, and which are the expressions of reported speakers. What gender issues do you see here? Language is very good stuff for insulting people with; what role do insults play in politics? What, also, does a sense of the comic, contribute to political journalism?

TEXT 33

Rebel MP attacks Blair's Stepford Wives

Labour's new women are 'automatons who have harmed lone parents'

By Jon Hibbs
Political Correspondent

Blair's babes are mainly "Stepford Wives", automatons with electronic chips implanted in their brains to keep them on the party line, according to a male critic from their own side.

Brian Sedgemore, Labour MP for Hackney South and Shoreditch, dismissed female backbenchers who did not join the rebellion against lone-parent benefit cuts last year as having done a disservice to women and children.

In a speech on the Government's policy towards fine art at the Tate Gallery in London, the Left-winger mounted an attack on New Labour. Joking that, like all Labour MPs, he had been programmed to stay "on message" for a thousand years without new batteries, he attacked the dozens of women who joined Labour's ranks last May.

"Then there's the Stepford Wives, that's those female, New Labour MPs who've had the chip inserted into their brains to keep them on message and who collectively put down women and children on the vote on lone-parent benefits," he said.

"Few of them have shown any interest in culture. I hesitate to say it but, in my opinion, a new Parliament replete with cultural inadequacies on the distaff side is no better than the old Parliament, replete as it was with artistic, testosterone morons."

The Stepford Wives was a sex-in-the-suburbs novel, later a film, about American husbands in search of the perfect wife, who kill their spouses and replace them with automatons programmed to do the housework and dedicate themselves to making their men happy.

Mr Sedgemore broadened his onslaught to include the Millennium Dome, suggesting that the £850 million project being overseen by Peter Mandelson, the minister without portfolio, was a waste of taxpayers' money and would go down in history as "Mandy's folly".

His remarks put him at odds with Tony Blair only weeks after he was formally reprimanded for his part in the Commons benefits revolt and put on notice about his behaviour in future.

Mr Sedgemore was one of three MPs to receive a personal dressing-down from Nick Brown, the Chief Whip, for writing an offensive letter of complaint about the "arm-twisters and goolie-crushers in the whips' office" and releasing it to the press.

Labour tried to play down his latest public outburst, insisting that the party did not want to make a martyr of the maverick.

"If he has decided he wants to dig his own grave and keeps on like this, something will happen sometime, but we don't want to give him the satisfaction of taking this seriously," said a spokesman for the leadership.

Following that hint, some women MPs declined to express their anger in case it fuelled the row. Helen Brinton, MP for Peterborough, said she was not interested in the comparison with the Stepford Wives.

But Margaret Hodge, elected MP for Barking in a 1994 by-election, made clear her displeasure. "Oh dear. He is a disappointed man who has been around too long. We have some of the best women in the '97 intake that have ever been in Parliament," she said.

Mr Sedgemore maintained that his criticisms were concerned solely with the arts but gave the game away when a BBC interviewer suggested later he should have got his speech approved in advance.

"The idea that a backbench Labour MP should run a speech past Millbank or Peter Mandelson is profoundly and deeply insulting – it is a kind of Leninist control and I believe in a pluralist democracy in which everyone puts their six-pennyworth in," Mr Sedgemore told Radio 4's *World at One*.

John Prescott, the Deputy Prime Minister, said Mr Sedgemore's comments were "deplorable". If the MP was making remarks like that, "they'd have great difficulty finding Brian's brain".

ACTIVITY 38

Lippy

Below is a selection of excerpts from a Leeds University women students' magazine called *Lippy* (October, 1997). Collectively the excerpts express young, feminist student voices on issues that concern them. The frequency with which interesting aspects of language appear is particularly interesting. First, read the texts and note specific language issues including the title itself. Next, answer the following questions:

1 What role is assigned to the reader? Are male readers excluded?
2 What preferred view of the world (ideology) lies behind the writing?
3 What specific details of language provide evidence for your answers to the above questions?

TEXT 34

EDITORIAL

Welcome to another issue of Leeds University Union Women's magazine (although you may not recognise it!). The name was changed due to complaints that 'Hysteria' was a derogatory term to use.

It is worth noting that the male equivalent title to 'Ward Sister' altered to become 'Charge Nurse'

WHAT I REALLY, REALLY WANT!

How many males would welcome their gender being absorbed into a female title?

I do think that if males and females are to continue to be biologically segregated by society, then at least the authorities should be consistent in their efforts and allow me to achieve a 'Mistress of Arts' degree upon successful completion of my course of study, as it is the more logical term in the circumstances (I really don't see 'Master' as being a serious option). 'Mistress' need not only communicate the negative connotations by which it is primarily known.

I was asked if I thought that women would welcome a change in titles. I replied that it should not be assumed that women approved of current provision and would need to be given an opportunity to discuss the issues, and consider available options. There has been a mixed response to the 'challenge'. I received nothing but supportive letters when the item was published in the *Guardian*, yet when the item was discussed on Radio Five Live, the three women (interviewed in the Students Union) whose responses were transmitted, all thought that I was being trivial, and one woman thought that I should not access study at these levels if I was 'so bothered by it'.

IT'S A WOMAN'S WORLD (YEAH, RIGHT!)

An example of where women don't have equal pay is in Hollywood. Four seasons into the programme of the X-Files and Gillian Anderson still earns only half the amount that David Duchovny gets. David Duchovny admittedly had more TV and film experience when the series began, but by this point shouldn't their salaries be a bit more balanced?

"Whether women are better than men I cannot say – but they are certainly no worse." – Golda Meir, Israeli Stateswoman and one time Prime Minister.

I do not wish them (women) to have power over men; but over themselves. – Mary Wollstonecraft.

"I'm not denying that women are foolish; God Almighty made them to match the men." – George Elliot (Mary Ann Evans), 19th Century English writer/author.

C*NT

(For us "can't" is a dirty word)

For many women can't is a dirty word.

It is a word which oppresses them and prevents them from achieving their true potential.

If people are continually told that they can't do something, then they begin to believe it. Many traditional views of women are full of can'ts. For example, if we are continually told that women can't work for the same wages as men do, then we are expected to settle for less.

Leeds University Union Women's Forum campaigns to show that women ***can***. Women ***can*** achieve what they want to. Women ***can*** be what they want to be, whether that is a single mother, a student or even a spice girl! Women ***can*** expect the same rights as men.

Past campaigns that Women's Forum have organised have included Zero Tolerance, International Women's Week and Reclaim the Night.

There is also a big fun side to Women's Forum which is also a social group. Past socials have included parties, visits to the steam baths in Harrogate and weekend breaks in the countryside.

If you want to get involved with Women's Forum in any way come to one of our meetings at:

The Women's Centre

Flat 14, 23 Cromer Terrace (Opposite Cromer Terrace Gym)

Thursdays 1–2pm every week. All women are welcome. For further information contact Helen Russell, Women's Officer on 231 4225, or pop up to the Exec Office in the Union.

MEN HAVE MADE POLITICS A COMBATIVE SPORT

"Sally Millard talked to New Labour women MPs about what the 'softer, more feminised' culture in the new parliament will mean for political life"

One of the most commented-on results of the election was the record number of women elected to parliament – 101 Labour MPs, 120 in all. While the tabloid headlines gave the new arrivals the patronising treatment ('Blair's babes', 'Backwenchers' etc), many commentators welcomed the fresh influx of women to a parliament which columnist Allison Pearson recently described as: 'So male that the very walls seem impregnated with testosterone' (*Evening Standard*, 27 March, 1997).

Anybody who feels passionately about an issue and is prepared to stand by what they think will realise that confrontation, debate and argument are part and parcel of getting your ideas across and convincing other people to take your side. This is what politics has traditionally been about, and it is the way the best ideas are developed. By pitting your wits and arguments against an opponent, both sides are forced to clarify an issue, justify their position, and in the process develop a more convincing case.
If New Labour have their way we will see little of this in the new parliament, as it smacks too much of an adversarial style now seen as out of date and unconstructive. Instead, a more friendly parliament requires politicians who are prepared to be polite and compromising, to 'wait and see' how the land lies before they speak. The 'feminised' Labour government has made clear its readiness to 'listen' and make compromises with the official opposition. But the new etiquette will ensure that MPs who want to challenge the government line will be open to accusations that they are being too 'masculine' in their style and upsetting the working atmosphere in the House. Tony Blair's plans to take the heat out of prime minister's question time symbolise New Labour's aim to sanitise common debate.

Reforming parliament to make it 'softer and more feminised' provides a handy rationale for removing controversial issues from the agenda and restricting debate. The notion of making parliament and politics more women-friendly also provides a pretext for imposing a strict new etiquette on public affairs, where everybody is effectively told to mind their p's and q's.

HOW FEMINIST ARE YOU?

2. You're getting on the bus to go to the Old Bar. The bus driver hands you your change with a smirk and says: "You don't get many of them to the pound". Do you:

a Wink at him and ask him what he is doing when he finishes work.
b Hit him with your hard back copy of Dale Spender's *Man Made Language*.
c Go crimson, sit down, and the next day write a letter to the bus company calling for appropriate action to be taken against the driver.

4. Your partner arrives and spends the next hour chatting up your best friend. Do you:

a Slag them off to everyone and then snog someone else.
b Tell them you feel fine about it because loving someone doesn't mean owning them.
c Ponder the pros and cons of sisterhood, while they disappear into the Harvey Milk Bar.

COMMENTARY

Quite clearly the purpose of the magazine is polemical, its primary audience being women and its primary purpose to express a feminist point of view in the face of prevailing masculinism. The magazine was originally entitled *Hysteria*, a title that seemed to have misfired. The word has, in fact, far more interesting meanings than the common association with uncontrolled screaming, laughter or crying. The word's original Greek meaning associated with the womb and its use in psychology to describe certain kinds of stress and paralysis never came through.

The new title, *Lippy*, is a deliberate choosing of a word usually used by males to put down females who speak up for themselves. Lippiness is an alternative to being 'dumb'. Notice again the ambiguity (dumb meaning 'unable to speak' and 'stupid'). Recall *The Times* report earlier which found that the British armed forces preferred women in war zones not to be interviewed.

The deliberate manipulation of language used about women, or of emphasising features thought 'typical' of women's talk is noticeable in the article headed, *What I Really, Really Want.* Regardless of what the article may be about, use of the repeated adverb is a provocative one in the face of studies that show women using this construction much more frequently than men. It was also topical in that it echoed a Spice Girls song.

Other linguistic foci of attention by the magazine itself are worth noting:

- *It's All in a Name* (a long standing expression of gender bias)
- *C*NT* (For us can't is a dirty word)
- *Men Have Made Politics A Combative Sport* (note how listening is associated with women and challenging speech with men, hence the statement, 'The "feminised" Labour government has made clear its readiness to "listen" and make compromises'.
- Note the suggestion in the semi-humorous questionnaire that you might just be carrying Dale Spender's *Man Made Language* to read on the bus!

Women as sex objects

So far you have looked at fairly explicit uses of language to discuss feminist issues and express a distinct gender voice. If you wish to read further on gender in modern texts, look at *Gender Voices* by David Graddol and Joan Swann (1990).

The next series of texts are mainly concerned with representations of women as sex objects and as symbols and ideals. Involved here are the imaginings, fantasies and desires we learn from our culture through art, myths, literature and which are exploitable by modern advertisers, newspapers and entertainment media.

ACTIVITY 39

Pretty woman

Look now at a passage from an influential and respected modern novel, *Possession: A Romance* by A. S. Byatt (1990). Make a note of references to female beauty, possession, property and sexual love.

What attitude do you detect in the author? What do you think concerns her? How do you think you are expected to respond?

Now write a brief fictional conversation piece of your own illustrating the way you see sexual relationships, power and possession.

TEXT 35

" 'Why do you go cold?' He kept his voice gentle.
'I – I've *analysed* it. Because I have the sort of good looks I have. People treat you as a kind of *possession* if you have a certain sort of good looks. Not lively, but sort of clear-cut and – '
'Beautiful.'
'Yes, why not. You can become a property or an idol. I don't want that. It kept happening.'
'It needn't.'
'Even you – drew back – when we met. I expect that, now. I use it.'
'Yes. But you don't want – do you – to be alone always. Or do you?'
'I feel as she did. I keep my defences up because I must go on *doing my work.* I know how she felt about her unbroken egg. Her self-possession, her autonomy. I don't want to think of that going. You understand?'
'Oh, yes.'
'I write about liminality. Thresholds. Bastions. Fortresses.'
'Invasion. Irruption.'
'Of course.'
'It's not my scene. I have my own solitude.'
'I know. You – you would never – blur the edges messily – '
'Superimpose – '
'No, that's why I – '
'Feel safe with me – '
'Oh no. Oh no. I love you. I think I'd rather I didn't.'
'I love you,' said Roland. 'It isn't convenient. Not now I've acquired a future. But that's how it is. In the worst way. All the things we – we grew up not believing in. Total obsession, night and day. When I see you, you look *alive* and everything else – fades. All that.'
...
So they took off their unaccustomed clothes, Cropper's multi-coloured lendings ... And very slowly and with infinite gentle delays and delicate diversions and variations of indirect assault Roland finally, to use an outdated phrase, entered and took possession of all her white coolness that grew warm against him, so that there seemed to be no boundaries ... "

ACTIVITY 40

Babewatch

The text and pictures below are taken from the *Radio Times* (17 January, 1998). Andrew Duncan has interviewed a top model, Caprice.

1 Read the passage noting any echoes from the Byatt excerpt.
2 What contribution do the pictures make?
3 What attitudes do you detect in Andrew Duncan?

TEXT 36

"IN BUSINESS TERMS I AM A PRODUCT. THE IMAGE I PORTRAY IS A FANTASY FIGURE"

In just over a year, she has rocketed to the top of the modelling world. But, insists CAPRICE, it's been more than just luck. Cool, calculated business acumen and the confidence to wear something outrageous in front of the cameras all contributed to her rapid rise

It is a tale of our times. A pneumatic Californian flibbertigibbet with intense ambition appears for a minute at the 1996 National TV Awards wearing flimsy Versace black lace covering skimpy knickers and thrusting décolletage. And, wham, bam, thank you ma'am, instant fame and £10,000 per appearance. She is "the world's hottest blonde", elevated to greater glory as the star, with Jonathan Ross, of a Pizza Hut commercial. She publicises National Wonderbra Week, returns to the TV awards last year with a diamond glued to her navel, and becomes known only by her Christian name. She even, heavens above, turns on the Bond Street Christmas lights, following in the hallowed footsteps of the late Princess of Wales and Liz Hurley.

Welcome Caprice Bourret, whose name roughly translates from the French as "drunken tantrum", an inappropriate sobriquet for a model with large blue eyes, lustrous blond hair, perfect teeth and complexion, interestingly poutable lips, and little-girl giggle befitting a former Miss Teen California with a body, insured for £500,000, encased today in Dolce and Gabbana crushed velvet trousers, white blouse, second-hand leather jacket and Chanel shoes. Like so many loved by the camera there is, to me, a disappointing vapidity about her in real life. Maybe we expect too much from an "image".

Possibly she's nervous because I have banished her amiable and efficient personal publicist Ghislain Pascal to another room, mobile-phoned to the hilt. We take tea in the Lanesborough Hotel library, London, and she turns on a recorder to ensure her words are not misconstrued. The churlish might suggest this is a waste of tape because our conversation is not, to say the least, of any geo-political significance.

"Honestly, with all my heart, I never anticipated the incredible reaction to that dress. It sounds ludicrous I became so well known because of it, but that's what happened. A lot of this business is timing. There are so many beautiful girls, you're bloody lucky to hit the right time." It helps if you're prepared to "sell" your body, I suppose. She looks blank. "Why would I sell my body? At the end of the day people love sex and looking at beautiful things, but there was nothing vulgar about the dress. Last year [the diamond coup], I wanted to create another sensation. It's wonderful to do these little stunts, but the sexy image will be dumped soon. You have to transform yourself, or you become stale and die. The public gets bored and says 'Next'. I've become complacent because I'm so happy living in England, but now I want to go for it in America. I'll give it my best shot, try to create hype. It's all a matter of semantics – that's one of my favourite sayings – but in business terms I am a product. The image I portray is a fantasy figure. I'm not a supermodel, nor really an actress. I'm a 'personality', a bit of everything. I built my own niche."

Putting on a brave front while modelling the goods during National Wonderbra Week

Commerical break: Jonathan Ross and Caprice discuss the finer aspects of Pizza Hut's stuffed crust

You have to be egotistical, too, I assume. "Gee, no one ever asked me that. I don't say I'm beautiful. It's everyone else who does. Do you understand? When I'm like this, with my hair tied back, very little make-up, I think I'm quite plain. This is the real me: down to earth, relaxed, a bit passive. But if someone wants me to be a sweet little girl or a sex goddess, I'll be it. That's my business. I love becoming a different person, but I'm very grounded and know exactly who I am."

"I'm overpaid, but you know what? I'm smiling and I don't care. I'd be a stupid schmuck to say, 'You shouldn't pay me this kind of money'."

The next phase of her career will be acting. "I'm good. I've always been an entertainer. As a child I'd have the family sit around the fireplace and watch as I did my little shows and sang my songs. I've been taking acting classes on and off for four years." She has made a travel series and was in a Channel 4 documentary, *Filthy Rich: Daddy's Girls*, with Tamara Beckwith, which some think showed her acting skills to great effect as she claimed she was "born" to polo fields and other luxuries. She says it was just a fun thing to do.

At the moment she is too busy to have a serious relationship. "That upsets me because it can be quite lonely. A lot of men want someone who is feminine, and to be in charge. It's difficult for them to have a woman making a substantial amount of money who's independent in her head. Although models are stereotyped, you can be pretty and have a brain as well. I believe people get an impression when they first meet me. Like, for instance, do you think I'm a complete ditz?" Her mobile telephone is trilling, the tea remains undrunk and Ghislain approaches to take her to a more lucrative assignment, so I leave the answer hanging in the air. *RT*

"PEOPLE LOVE BEAUTIFUL THINGS. THERE WAS NOTHING VULGAR ABOUT THAT DRESS"

The Versace dress that catapulted Caprice into the headlines

COMMENTARY

Notice the way in which Caprice speaks of herself as a product and a fantasy. But how far is the article spun to give prominence to this?

Duncan's technique is to weave what Caprice actually said into an article rather than present a straight question and answer text. This gives him the opportunity to contextualise her words as he sees fit. Aware that last sentences are often giveaways in articles of this kind, how do you interpret the last sentence here?

In Byatt's novel there is a feeling that despite the fact that it is fiction, the author is concerned with truths about human love and sexuality. Her writing is serious, disturbing even. She has a carefully controlled yet deep concern for the fate of her characters.

Duncan's writing belongs to the 'infotainment' genre mentioned earlier, in which the discourse appears to play with, and perhaps even reinforce stereotypes. Do you detect any cynicism? scepticism? Any serious criticism, implicitly or explicitly, of the business value of sex objects?

Women in advertising

The use of female beauty either as sex object or as an ideal in modern advertising is only too well known as a topic of gender studies. The 1990s have seen a flood of market research and academic investigations into the role of women in all kinds of advertising for both men and women. In 1992, the Proceedings of the Marketing Education Group Conference, contained an update of the trends at the end of the 1980s and the beginning of the 1990s. In 1994, a working paper by Wood and Griffiths from University of Salford, concluded their research summary as follows:

'All researchers appear to agree that advertisers have not kept pace with the changing image of woman, and still portray women in traditional roles such as housewives, or as sex objects, looking to their husband/partner for approval and guidance'.

On the next page is an example from the 1940s of a traditional female image in advertising. It appeared in the *Women's Institute* magazine and is now a classic in its depiction of approval-seeking wifeliness and pipe smoking, male smugness.

'Read' this illustration in the light of Deborah Cameron's comments on pages 58–9.

Studies of advertisements that did portray women in more progressive roles found that progressive women responded very positively to such advertisements while women with more traditional attitudes had no objection. This has led some advertisers into adopting more progressive strategies in the portrayal of sex roles, since it appears to attract progressive women without alienating traditional women. Despite this however, Woods and Griffiths found that in the mid 1990s, women were three times more likely to be portrayed as sex objects than men. They also show that

"You little Spendthrift"

"Listen! Jim! These £3 worth of woollies cost me 13/–."

"What? That lot thirteen bob?"

"Yes—all on my wonderful Cymbal Knitter. Easy as anything—I've turned out this jumper since tea—All these are for us. Then, Jim, I start on my first £10 order!"

"£10 order?"

"Yes, Mrs. Evans and her friend saw some of my work to-day and gave me a £10 order on the spot. They were astounded at the quality of the work, and said they would have to pay double my prices in the West End. *And I make* £4-10-0. But, Jim, this is the best news. Even if I don't want to sell to friends and shops I am sure of a regular income each week from the Cymbal Company. Here is their guarantee to buy at good prices all the work I care to send them for three years."

What about you, dear reader? There's no room to explain here how you can have a regular extra income of your own and have beautiful things to wear for next to nothing, so we have provided the coupon below for you to use. You have everything to gain and nothing to lose by posting it.

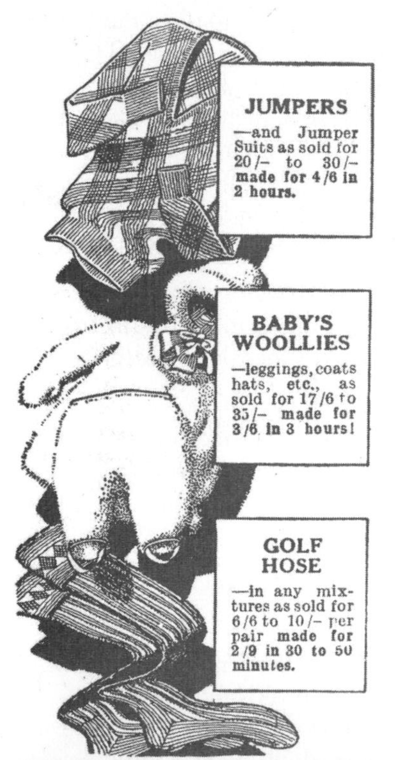

Readers in London should call at the demonstration Salon at 90 Borough High Street (just over London Bridge)

COUPON

Fill in and post (½d. stamp on an unsealed envelope will do) to Cymbal Ltd., Cymbal House, 90 Borough High Street, London, S.E.1.

Please send me free and post free in plain packing your 32-page illustrated Book which explains all about the Cymbal Knitter, and shows all the kinds of garments that can be made with it even by anyone who doesn't know how to knit. Explain also very clearly how I could be assured of a regular income under your spare-time salary plan. It is clearly understood, of course, that sending this coupon places me under no obligation whatsoever.

NAME ....

ADDRESS ....

H. A. C. 4.

other researches confirm that in the late 1980s and early 1990s, men were more likely to be the central character of car advertisements. Their own research into 1990's car advertisements however discovered a tendency for women to be presented as central characters. in other words, more car advertisements are targeted at independent women.

ACTIVITY 41

Ask before you borrow it

The article and picture below were published in the *Sun*, four years after the Woods and Griffiths study (29 July, 1998). Read it and make your own observations. You could write a letter to the editor saying what you think. Keep additional linguistic issues, such as the suggestion of taboo words in advertising, separate from the gender issues here.

TEXT 37

One of these ads is officially offensive. Can you guess which?

CAR APPEAL . . . the Nissan Micra advertising campaign featured a hard-hitting message – but how much did the public appreciate the joke?

These two adverts both use sex to sell their products. But which one is the more offensive?

Is it model Eva Herzigova – pouting seductively in her uplifting Wonderbra – calling out to passers-by: "Hello Boys"?

Or the Nissan Micra car ad – slogan "Ask Before You Borrow It" – featuring a man holding his crotch as though he has just been kneed by its woman owner?

A shock report reveals that the public considered the Micra ad to be offensive while the bra campaign was "successful and memorable."

Both men and women described it as humorous. Men considered it tantalising while women said it

showed a colleague in control poking fun at men.

But the Nissan ad, meant to show how women can make their own decision when it comes to which cars they like, was considered objectionable by both sexes.

The Advertising Standards Authority, which commissioned the report, say the public are increasingly concerned at the way companies are trying to shock to sell their products and they don't like men or women being portrayed as sex objects.

So how did Wonderbra manage to get away with it while Nissan didn't?

ASA spokesman Chris Read explains: "The Wonderbra ad shows you can get away with a sexy ad as long as it is humorous. Nissan pushed the barriers that bit further and people found it unfunny and offensive."

Both adverts were produced by top London agency TBWA.

Managing director Neil Christie says: "The results of the survey surprise me. The Wonderbra ad is probably the most famous poster campaign of the last ten years. It took a subject normally associated with women's magazines and made it noticed in a direct and sexy way.

"The Micra ad is also provocative but in a different way. It is aimed more at the people the ad wants to talk to. Some people might not like it, but it's probably not for them."

The ASA say companies have to be wary when pushing traditional taboos of advertising to the limit.

The growing trend to show gays and lesbians is also causing alarm.

The Impulse body spray commercial – showing a woman bumping into the man of her dreams only to see him wander off holding hands with another man – did not work with the public.

And a poster campaign for jeans which featured two apparently naked women about to kiss brought a large number of complaints.

References to drug taking, rude gestures and the use of swear words were also not liked.

More than 1,000 people were questioned for the ASA report, which found people were becoming more offended rather than less by swearing than they were two years ago. And they were more prepared to express their annoyance. More than eight in ten now want to see bad language banned.

The main cause of offence was that many ads were seen as not suitable for children.

Almost one in five people thought ads set a bad example to youngsters, especially when posters showing sexually-explicit images were put up near schools.

References to drugs also caused offence. One example was the Sony Playstation advert for its game Coolboarders II, which urged "My body aches for Powder, I need the rush. Have to get higher than last time."

Chris Read says: "Sometimes one event can result in a huge shift in public opinion about images in advertising – such as the Jamie Bulger case or Dunblane. They led to an increase in complaints almost overnight about violent imagery and the portrayal of children."

ASA director general Matti Alderson adds: "There are clearly a number of areas where the advertising industry should continue to be wary. But overall, standards of advertising remain high and the numbers of adverts withdrawn as a result of complaints are very low."

COMMENTARY

The whole article is an exemplary bit of journalism regardless of the content. Notice how the title, in the form of a gameshow puzzle, sets up the whole article by involving the reader in a possible element of surprise. Notice though some lexical choices:

- the use of 'sex' when it means 'female' or 'female body'
- the use of 'colleague' to describe a woman 'poking fun at men'
- 'It is aimed more at people the ad wants to talk to' (a remarkably astute discourse remark by an advertiser)
- 'The growing trend to show gays and lesbians is also causing alarm' (what ideology lies behind this, especially when it is contextualised by the preceding sentence about taboos and the later references to drugs, swearing and unsuitability for children?).

Agency

An aspect of discourse analysis not yet raised is the question of agency. Agency is a grammatical term referring to the actor or agent who performs the action of the verb (The cat sat on the mat while the dog slept on the hearth – 'cat' and 'dog' are the agents of the actions). 'Agency' as a term in stylistics and discourse analysis identifies who did what to whom (or had it done unto them! This is passivity or passivisation). The interesting thing about the Micra advert is that the agent is not present in the advert at all, though by intertextual reference, we know who she is from the TV advert. Whether women are portrayed as initiating agents in an advert or as recipients of male action or approval is an issue that will recur in the next series of texts.

ACTIVITY 42

The car's the star

Below are seven car advertisements featuring women. All but the Corsa advert appeared in the summer of 1997. The Corsa advert appeared in the early 1990s and has been included because of complaints of sexism. If, as research, suggests, the ideology is shifting in favour of equality of sexual respect for women, then the adverts appeared at a time when more car advertisements than ever were being targeted at women as potential, independent purchasers. Look at the adverts and describe in your own written words how women are portrayed in each one. As in all these activities, it isn't enough to think and talk about the texts. You need to practise getting sometimes complex thoughts into clear written statements that will show an examiner that you know what you are doing.

Some questions you could ask are:

- What social/cultural conventions are being invoked by the advertiser?
- What roles are assigned to characters in the advertisements? What conclusions can be drawn about the social and power relations between them?
- What is the taken-for-granted view of life that is being contested in the advert? Are women, for example, being portrayed in more proactive roles?

Finally, make sure you have identified in detail the linguistic and the pictorial evidence that enable you to see what kind of discourse is going on.

THE NEW RENAULT CLIO PANACHE £7,895
YOU'VE EITHER GOT IT OR YOU HAVEN'T

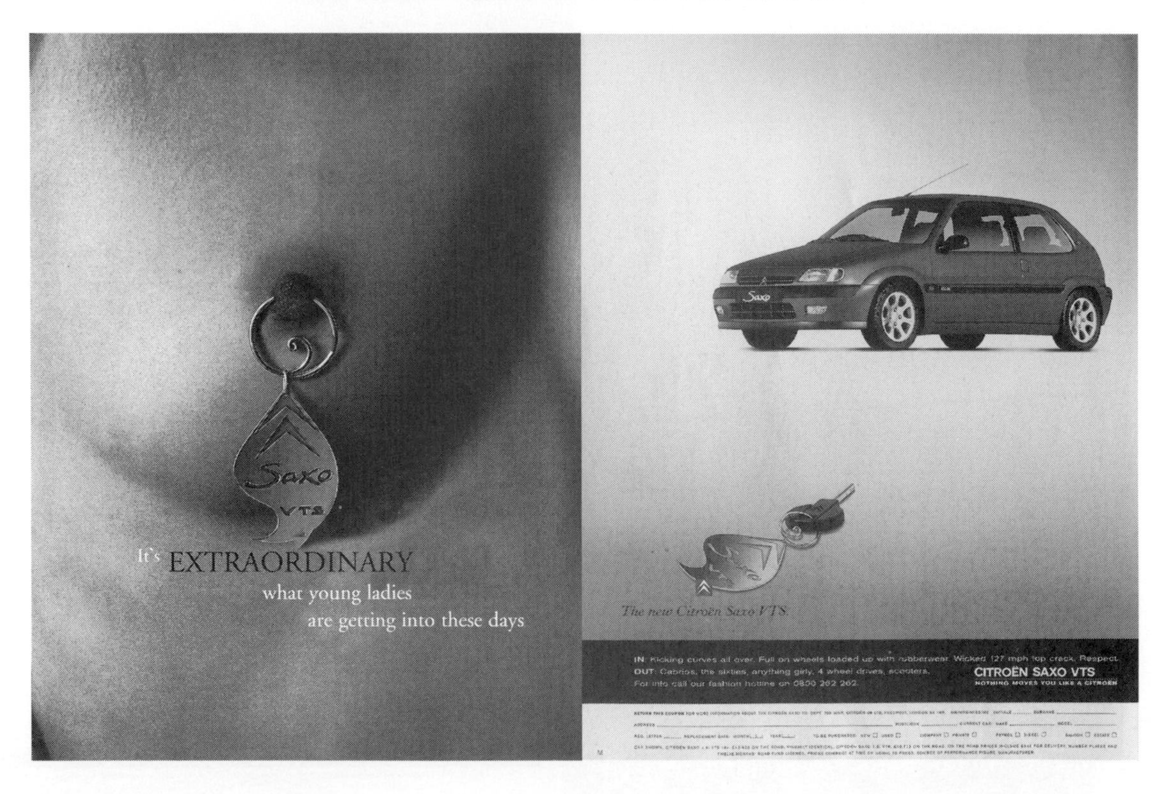

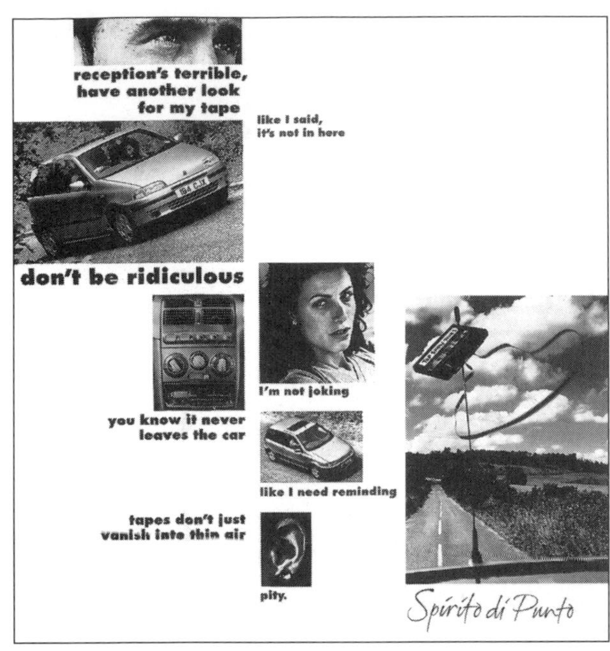

Text above reads: 'The Hyundai Coupe'. With a drag co-efficient of 0.33, even the wind can't resist it.

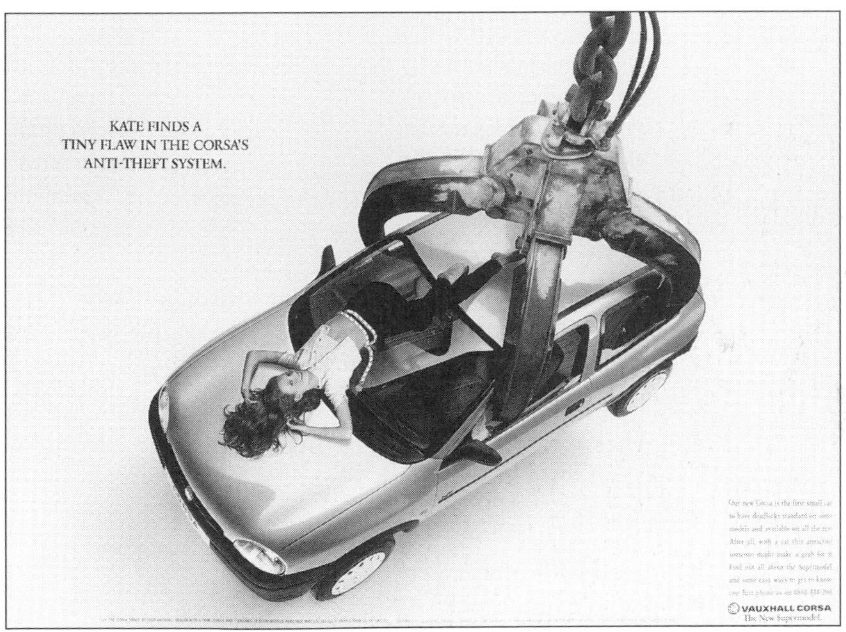

COMMENTARY

You will have made a number of observations and gathered lots of data. You could set out your findings in a table as shown below. We have added the specific details about the cars and the magazines in which they appeared.

Car	Description of advert	Roles	Evidence
Nissan Micra (*New Woman*, 1997)	Female owner dislikes male borrowing car; gets own back; feeds man dog food.	Proactive	Strong image; use of imperative; curvaceous, aggressive image of woman; submissive male.

Fiat Punto (*Radio Times*, 1997)	Female passenger dislikes male's taste in music and prevents it from being played.	Proactive	Sophisticated narrative text and narrative pictures.
Daihatsu Hijet (*Radio Times*, 1997)	Male thinks he is 'stud' because he has four children, and family car. Female smiles knowingly.	Proactive but appears passive	Irony; three adjectives, 'great, big, hunky'; Note the smile.
Renault Clio (*Radio Times*, 1997)	Car foregrounded. Couple having romantic picnic in background.	Neutral	The car, the male and the female all have PANACHE.
Citroen Saxo (*Marie Claire*, 1997)	Female nipple pierced with keyring and car's name. Picture of car where other breast would be.	Passive, but appears proactive	Provocative; written and pictorial language suggest independence but woman is sex object.
Hyundai Coupe	Viewer resists looking at beautiful woman on backseat to look at car.	Passive	Key notion is being 'irresistible'; woman resisted, car isn't.
Vauxhall Corsa	Supermodel Kate Moss lies on top of advertised car while claw from crane grabs rear of car.	Passive	Contradiction; mismatch between written pictorial messages of improved security and quite unrelated sex object role of the model.

There are many more aspects of car advertising that could be examined here. There is the theme of possession, for example, words such as 'curves' and 'sporty' or 'sporting' occur in more than one advert.

Because words belong to families, advertisers can cause the readers to think the right word by triggering it. When they use the word 'resist', the reader thinks, 'irresistible'.

Sexual references are fairly frequent:

- 'loaded with rubberwear'
- 'infallible in the sack'
- 'alluring'
- 'curves'.

Fashion and discourse

The next series of texts come from fashion magazines. The two on the left are from the fashion section of *Marie Claire* (1997), the one on the top right is from *New Woman* (1997). They belong to a genre that is not strictly advertising but is not purely a review either. Both magazines are written for fashionable consumers and the discourse is an influential, trend setting kind of writing that boosts sales indirectly.

ACTIVITY 43

Model girls

Study the pictures, making detailed notes on your perceptions of the models. What ideas do you associate with each one? Get into words as much as you can, however fleeting your thoughts and impressions may be. Remember that your mind will be wording and imaging far more quickly than you can write.

Ask yourself, for example:

1. what role has the woman been assigned? Proactive? Passive?
2. what is the visual evidence for your interpretation?
3. what is the verbal evidence?

sheer
elegance

flaunt your femininity: sexy sheer chiffons and delicate lace bring a soft touch to summer daywear. From floaty layers, trimmed with ribbon and lace, to provocative silk lingerie paired with structured separates. Photograph by Patrick Demarchelier

COMMENTARY

Here are some comments on the *Marie Claire* pictures. See how they compare with yours, and then see if they add anything to your 'reading' of the picture from *New Woman.*

Both *Marie Claire* pictures are embedded in a journalistic context. It is important to recognise the discourse genre here: direct journalism, indirect advertising. A significant contextual factor mentioned in the article is that at the catwalk showing, the fashion industry was heavily criticised for making the models look like heroin addicts. Their faces were gaunt with dark, smudged eye make-up. In other words, there was strong objection by some people to the roles assigned to the models and to the social conventions being invoked or flouted. Some, however, did not object.

The first picture is accompanied by the words: 'The frill of it' and, 'Ruffles add a romantic edge to dresses and skirts.' There is a pun here (frill/thrill) but notice that there is also a pun on the word 'edge'. The combination of the word 'edge' (meaning 'edgy') and 'thrill' seem to complement the sense of nervous, dangerous excitement conveyed by the make-up and the opening exclamation, 'the frill of it'. The word 'romantic' (which implies nice sex) is almost incongruous here, unless a dark, dangerous kind of romanticism is implied. Note that the model has been asked to look directly at the camera, and that in addition to the heavy eye make-up, her cheek has been given a shiny, bruised texture. The sentence functions of the accompanying words are exclamation plus statement (or declarative).

The picture underneath is accompanied by the words:

- 'sheer elegance'
- 'Flaunt your femininity: sexy, sheer chiffons and delicate lace bring a soft touch of summer daywear. From floaty layers, trimmed with ribbon and lace, to, provocative silk lingerie paired with structured separates.'

There is a fair amount of conventional fashion advertising copy here: 'delicate lace' and 'sheer elegance'. The alliterations in the first lines are routinely obvious, but professionals know they are expected as part of the act.

The functional phrase 'structured separates' does however sit uncomfortably with 'delicate lace'. The sentence functions in the advert are again imperative plus declarative. Note that the words between 'From …' and '… separates' are verbless, the kind of minor sentence popular in advertising.

The model has been told to look at the camera but her posture turns away defensively, as though physical violence threatens. Make-up is very similar to that in the first picture, but under her right eye is a smudge suggesting that she may have been crying. Certainly there is more than a suggestion here of a feminine role that is passive, tearful, weak, victimised and drug addicted.

In terms of influencing fashion preferences and generating powerful associations of words and images, the magazine *Marie Claire* is successful, but there are remarkable ambiguities in this kind of discourse. There is a mixture of socially conventional, romantic, sexy femininity and socially unconventional drug addiction. The contrast shows between the words and pictures and in the words themselves. A fair question raised is:

How far are the models portrayed as sex objects – and sado-masochistic ones at that? How far are they portrayed as autonomous women?

The magazine's writers can claim that they are reflecting and reviewing what they saw on the catwalk and that it is their job to make informative fashion journalism as exciting and as provocative as possible.

Ultimately it is in the reader's own imagination that the power of the magazine's words and images have their effect, which is why some kind of critical analysis is necessary. Australian writers refer to it as 'critical literacy'; Norman Fairclough calls it 'critical language awareness'; to Deborah Cameron, it is 'verbal hygiene'. It is not so much a matter of juggernaut media brainwashing people; it is more complex than that. It is true that we use our judgement when we read, but it is still worthwhile knowing just what it is we are accepting or questioning.

The *Spice Girls* phenomenon

The final group of texts in this chapter centre on the Spice Girls. Please don't be put off if you can't stand their music. What you will be investigating is the Spice Girls as a media/consumer phenomenon who have made feminist issues part of their publicity. They have undoubtedly hit commodity marketing and the media hype machine in a big way even to the extent of being included in 1998 dictionaries.

ACTIVITY 44

From Manpower to Girl Power

The word 'manpower', as opposed to 'horsepower', belongs very much to the Industrial Revolution. It denotes the change in employment patterns which occurred with the development of mining and factory industries during the 19th century. In the early 1990s the term was still used to describe a government network of employment agencies, *Manpower Services*, and later *Manpower* became the name of a private sector employment agency. It should be remembered that both organisations found work for men and women. The use of the word 'man' in relation to work continues in such terms as 'man hours', 'men at work', 'manning', but is under threat as words like 'chairperson' replace 'chairman'.

Look up the word 'manpower' in the *Oxford English Dictionary* on CD-Rom if possible or in a large dictionary. Look up also uses of the word 'man' as a verb on its own and in such compounds as 'manhandle'.

Now look up the word 'girl'. You may be surprised to learn that its original meaning covered boys as well as girls. Think too of some of the ways in which the word is used today: 'a mere slip of a girl'; 'girlies'; 'good-time girl'; 'girl crazy' and so on. Sort them out into those with positive values and connotations and those with negative. What are the essential distinctions between the meaning of 'girl' and 'woman'?

A Brief History of Womanpower

The word 'manpower' denotes a key concept in the growth of the factory system in the early 19th century. Whilst there was enough work for the manpower, woman's role was essentially in the home. Poorer women however needed to work as well as run a home and family.

1861 26% of total female population over age 15 worked, mostly in domestic service, 'woman's work'
1870 education had slowly made it more and more possible for girls to get work in teaching, nursing, clerical assistance
1901 fewer worked in domestic service and more in shops and factories, which paid better wages for shorter hours, and gave more independence
1910 Women's Movement won free milk, school meals, midwives
1914–1918 during the war, economic necessity made it socially acceptable for women to do men's work but for lower wages. After the war, despite 500,000 being unemployed, women were not willing to return to domestic service.
1918 women over age of thirty gained the vote
1919 Women's Charter asserted rights to work and leisure
1926 Hadow Report on education nevertheless emphasised domestic work for girls
1933 a Rally of women's organisations proclaimed right of married women to work
1934 a similar rally demanded equal pay for equal work
1930s Women were employed because they were cheaper than men
1939–45 war again made it socially acceptable for women to do men's work
1941 Government compelled to conscript women into factory work because they were proving reluctant to volunteer – they were still paid less than men
1951 there began great expansion in service industries which led to many part-time openings for women. It was becoming acceptable for all married women to work. 12% worked part-time
1960 big increase in number of University places for women
1970 Sex Discrimination Act passed; implemented in 1975
1970 first conference of Women's Liberation Movement
1981 40% of women in part-time work
1993 65% of women in part-time work
1997 Spice Girls' manifesto on Girl Power
1998 the first woman was appointed to command a warship

Just like a girl

In 1994, Susan Sharpe published *Just Like a Girl: How Girls Learn to be Women* (Penguin). It is a book you will find worth reading not only for its intrinsic interest but also for Sharpe's interview method which has distinct possibilities for language study coursework.

She researched the attitudes and hopes of teenage girls, noting that 'many girls in the 1990s remain reluctant to identify themselves as feminist … and (that) there is a tendency to assume more change than has actually taken place'. There is an awareness that whilst feminists have brought about some legal change, less change in traditional attitudes is evident.

Sharpe quotes the views of teenagers:

'Feminism is still relevant but not so much now. I think things are changing a lot . . . They (men) don't need women now to say there shouldn't be a divide because men've realised it now, everyone is changing. It's a lot better.' (Teresa)

Despite this optimistic voice, Sharpe concludes that, although men acknowledge women's rights and equality, such recognition is rarely translated into behaviour:

'With their backs to the wall, many men are put into a position of defending what they have.'

The need now is for 'young women to demand and create these equal opportunities'.

And along came the Spice Girls in 1997! With a mixture of personal conviction, youthful enthusiasm and media hype they voiced a new, aggressive teenage girl power. In their book, *Girl Power* (1997) they say:

'Feminism has become a dirty word. Girl Power is just a '90s way of saying it. We can give feminism a kick up the arse. Women can be powerful when they show solidarity.'

It is not too important how the book was written, how many of the Spice Girls were actually teenagers at the time, or who might have been pulling some of the strings. More important is the symbolic power they achieved. Newspaper headlines still use the language trick of attaching 'power' to any group who have voiced an opinion: Kids Power; Pensioner Power; Granny Power; Player Power (in football); Boyz Power; Dads Power have all appeared. The symbolic power of the Spice Girls was achieved from a solid financial base.

Released in 1996, the album *Spice* had sold eleven million copies by the summer of 1997 (*Marketing Focus*). The *Sun* newspaper calculated their gross income (1997) as follows:

album sales	8.6 m
Spiceworld: The Movie	5 m
writer royalties	4 m
singles sales	2.6 m
merchandising	1.5 m
TV show	1 m
live appearances	1 m
Pepsi deal	1 m
Channel 5 launch	1–2 m

Huge popular appeal and this kind of financial success gained the Spice Girls three kinds of power:

- influence, control and status in the media
- force in shaping the ideas of young people
- a new colloquial emphasis on the words 'spice' and 'girl power' which associated them with a lifestyle and ideology.

Many writers have observed that communications media have replaced church and school as moral educators by virtue of their popular influence rather than their authority. In one of their songs, *the Spice Girls* deliver an educational message about safe sex:

'Be a little wiser baby, put it on, put it on
'Cause tonight is the night when two become one'

ACTIVITY 45

The Spice Code

Below is a sequence of texts that express the Spice Girl manifesto or code. Read them and summarise the outlook on life, the ideology, conveyed in their explicit campaign and expressed in the discourse.

TEXT 38

GIRL POWER IS WHEN ...

You help a guy with his bag
You and your mates reply to wolf whistles by shouting "Get your arse out!"

You wear high heels and think on your feet

You know you can do it and nothing's going to stop you

You don't wait around for him to call

You stick with your mates and they stick with you

You're loud and proud even when you've broken out in spots

You believe in yourself and control your own life

GIRL
POWER

I'VE GOT GIRL POWER BECAUSE ...

"... I was engaged, but broke away and found myself and my friends when I realised he wasn't right for me."

" ... I play football even though a lot of people turn their noses up at girls' football."

" ... I expect an equal relationship where he does just as much washing-up as I do (if not more)!"

" ... I appreciate that I am mixed race and I follow my own roots."

" ... I try and make the best of what I've got – even if I'm small, I think tall."

GIRL
POWER

COMMENTARY

The Spice Girls define personal power in two ways: preferred attitudes and preferred behaviours. Their code may be summarised as follows:

Attitudes	Behaviour	Examples
Know yourself	Make the best of what you've got	
Self-belief	Break female stereotypes	Play football Help men with bags
Control your life	Be assertive	Be loud/proud; reply to wolf whistles
	Be a little naughty	Swear
	Be fashionable	Wear high heels
	Have a rewarding relationship	Don't wait for him to call – leave him
	Develop friendships	Be a shoulder to cry on
Be unstoppable	Think on your feet	

A key element of the *Spice Girls'* concept of 'Girl Power' is controlling your own life which means being assertive and naughty. The use of the word 'naughty' could partly be a desire to shock but partly a turning to advantage a word traditionally used by men to put women in their place by treating them as children.

Being naughty and debunking conformity are almost the same thing in Spice Girl discourse. They debunk conformity by both verbal and pictorial means. The Christmas message for example, 'Spice it up' is very similar to other 1990s catchphrases: 'mad for it', 'get a life', having 'attitude', 'living it large'. It is not exactly clear what these terms mean in themselves, but reinforced by visual images and hit songs, they are the idiom of a lifestyle. Pictures are an important part of the *Spice Girls'* marketing; they illustrate what being naughty, assertive, debunking and spicey all mean. Their pictures give the words their special meaning, and can be analysed in five components:

Key Component	Signal Being Sent
1 Facial expression	Smiles, allure, 'mean and moody'
2 Posture	Provocative, direct look at the camera, 'in your face'
3 Dress Code	Fashionable and skimpy
4 Environment	On and around the bed
5 Overall impression	Relaxed, fun loving, proactive

You may recollect from TV and newspapers how the *Spice Girls* refuse to co-operate with the conventions of pop interview techniques and proved very difficult to interview on anyone else's terms but their own.

An example of how advertising media feed on catchphrases is illustrated by the following car advert. In general it is an unremarkable, even dull advertisement but notice the word 'noughty', a pun on the *Spice Girls'* 'naughty'. Here, the word has a range of meanings: being slightly improper, having a spirit of adventure, being eye-catching and sporty.

You have to decide for yourself where the Spice Girls fit into your perspective on feminism. You may think they are simply entertainers, media commodities, exploiting words like 'naughty' for effect, knowing how eagerly (and profitably) the effect will be consumed.

How would you distinguish their code from a modern male code? You would need to analyse texts from *Loaded*, *FHM* and *GQ* to get some idea of a media-generated male equivalent.

We conclude this section with two items from newspapers, illustrating different responses to the *Spice Girls*. What are they saying explicitly and implicitly?

TEXT 39

Women seize power at work

Mild-mannered men are taking the back seat as a new generation of "superwomen" come to power in offices and factories all over Britain.

As men are becoming meeker and less macho, an era of girl power is bringing revolution to the workplace.

Unlike their mothers, who were often shy and unassuming, today's women are eager to demand their share of the action.

And growing numbers of men are suffering traditionally female stress problems such as anorexia and bulimia.

Top management consultant Dr Robert McHenry of Oxford Psychologists Press, a company which specialises in personality tests, says there is evidence women are hungry for power.

He said: "Women under 30 are more likely than their mothers to describe themselves as independent, assertive and competitive. These are characteristics traditionally perceived as leadership qualities usually displayed by men."

The sex revolution is reflected in the answers people give in millions of psychometric tests – the questionnaires many firms use at interview to assess candidates' personalities.

Dr McHenry said: "Men under 30 describe themselves as less aggressive and more sensitive than older men – who have accused them of being wet."

Young women now joining the workforce grew up with Mrs Thatcher as a role model – and are more at home with the idea that men are the underdogs and women should be in charge.

As they mature, more and more will find themselves in top management jobs – putting paid to traditional sex discrimination.

Dr McHenry said women are now better equipped for senior roles as they combine the assertiveness of their fathers with the team instinct of their mothers.

From The Huddersfield Weekly News, 19 August 1997

TEXT 40

The problem with Girl Power

by Beatrix Campbell

So Svengali's girls have spurned the man who made them. The girls have given up their guru. Music industry moguls predict the decline of the Spice Girls now that they have decided to dispense with the services of their magician-manager Simon Fuller.

"They've bitten the hand that feeds them," complains one "industry expert" whose comments are an illuminating inversion of the ingredients of the Spice Girls' spectacular success. Who was feeding whom? Who are the Spice Girls anyway? By this account, Simon Fuller is really the Spice Girls, he is their breadwinner and they merely mime his every move and mutter his every motto. But surely it was the Spice Girls who made Fuller's living. If reports of a £10 million settlement between Fuller and the band are accurate, they earned his fortune.

The story of the split between the Spice guy and his gals is a parable for our time. If newspaper reports of his brilliant but single-minded management style are to be believed, here's a man who thinks he owns his workers, who thinks that when he patrols the private lives as well as the public performances of some of the hottest women in the world, he is only protecting them. This is a story of professional patriarchy. The Spice Girls weren't just managed by Fuller, they were exhausted by him. After two years, they were said to be worn out by their phenomenal work rate.

Of course, the relationship was symbiotic, as those between performers and impresarios, like proletarian and capitalists, usually are. But the response to the split suggests that the Spice Girls are seen as shadows, virtual performers whose stardom will wilt without Fuller's wand.

The response to their bid for freedom tells a larger story, however, about the policing of powerful and public women. It is not simply that the band's success depended on playing "Simon says", but that some commentators seem to think that without management, women become literally unmanageable. By being themselves, they become unruly, wanton, as if self-possession poses too great a threat to the public realm. When the Spice Girls' tour of South Africa brought them face to face with Nelson Mandela and Prince Charles, there was talk that they'd gone too far, that these encounters had gone to their heads, and in no time they were sacking their manager. But maybe what they had learnt was that the man's need was greater than theirs – and that, of course, is unbearable.

From The *Guardian*, 11 November 1997

Summary

In this chapter you have explored a variety of texts that raiser gender issues, whether it be women at work, advertising cars and fashion or the creation of a very persuasive lifestyle code for teenage girls. It should be evident that the reader's own imagination plays a big part in the effectiveness of the discourse of these texts, especially those advertising or exploiting, or both.

Texts are extraordinarily selective, as indeed is all language use. They may appear to be connected with real life, and sometimes are, but real life is so much more. What a text does is to make you see things in a particular way and follow a particular kind of discourse. As an A-Level English Language student you have to get inside the text to discover what it is saying and then step outside in order to see it in its social context and to take stock of how it has worked in your mind.

One very good way of taking control of a text, is to consider how you might edit and represent the text for another purpose and another audience. We suggest that you regard all the texts in this chapter as source material for a case study, a desk study or a re-casting exercise, whichever syllabus you are following.

Your new context is imaginative radio broadcasting and your task is to produce a fifteen minute programme for BBC Radio 2. Your brief is to write a script based on a good cross section of the texts in this chapter that will allow different voices to come through. You must however have something to say yourself: a theme, a polemic or a storyline. This will help you weave together parts of other people's texts and enable you to say what you want to say, in the way you want to say it.

Be as imaginative as you like but ensure that you are producing your own discourse about gender in modern times and not somebody else's. Choose your own title and make sure your instructions to the presenters are clear at every stage. Remember too that your audience will be a listening audience.

5 You and Yours: Language, Power and Citizenship

In Chapters Three and Four you looked at ways in which powerful social influences construct, through language, cultural (lifestyle) values and our ideas of gender. In this final chapter you will explore how ideas of citizens' rights and responsibilities are constructed by traditions, politicians, businesses and pressure groups. You will investigate the kind of discourse used and, as ever, look at lexical choices, implied meanings and the contexts in which texts are produced.

After an initial consideration of the idea of citizenship, a series of texts will be presented to you in the following sequence:

- two views of citizenship from W. H. Auden and The Institute of Citizenship Studies
- government views in relation to social welfare and the 'New Deal'
- ethical business policies produced by Tesco, Somerfield, The Body Shop and Nestlé
- moral crusades abroad and at home (Amnesty International and the campaign of Mrs Frances Lawrence).

Passport please

Most people rarely, if ever, read their passports, except to check that they are up to date. However, passports are worth reading as a stylistics exercise because they are very powerful documents. If you own a British passport, for example, you will find yourself officially described as a British citizen. There is also a note explaining 'Citizenship' and 'National Status'. Besides being an abstract noun (one of the many ending in '-ship') 'citizenship' has rather stodgy connotations. But change the usual perspective and it becomes a much more interesting study. Look at citizenship from the point of view expressed in the book *Trainspotting* (see page 43): 'Choose DIY and wondering who the fuck you are on a Sunday morning'. There's a nice combination here of consumerism, home improvement, being a good conformist and yet underneath it all, a mind that still asks serious questions about life. Who am I? Is this what life is all about? There must be more to it? Citizenship is part of this debate. Throughout history, most often in times of crisis, people have had recourse to the word 'citizenship': Aristotle, the writers of Magna Carta,

Machiavelli, Rousseau, Marx, Hitler, among many have all had a go at defining it. It's a favourite word of politicians: Margaret Thatcher, John Major and Tony Blair have all used it.

ACTIVITY 46

A poet's view

Below is a poem by W. H. Auden, written in 1939. It pre-echoes the sentiment in the *Trainspotting* excerpt and also the questioning of conformity expressed by the *Spice Girls*. The tone is of course very different.

Read the poem which, in contrast to political uses of the word 'citizen', is full of irony. Ironic discourse is very subversive because it works by implication, making you state the meaning of the poem rather than spelling it out.

Describe in writing, just how Auden uses language to create this ironic condemnation of modern life. When you have done this compare Auden's discourse with that of *Trainspotting*. Is the Auden poem old-fashioned or still relevant?

TEXT 41

The Unknown Citizen

To JS/07/M/378
This Marble Monument is Erected by the State

He was found by the Bureau of Statistics to be
One against whom there was no official complaint,
And all the reports on his conduct agree
That, in the modern sense of an old-fashioned word, he was a saint,
For in everything he did he served the Greater Community,
Except for the War till the day he retired
He worked in a factory and never got fired,
But satisfied his employers, Fudge Motors Inc.
Yet he wasn't a scab or odd in his views,
For his Union reports that he paid his dues,
(Our report on his Union shows it was sound)
And our Social Psychology workers found
That he was popular with his mates and liked a drink.
The Press are convinced that he bought a paper every day
And that his reactions to advertisements were normal in every way.
Policies taken out in his name prove that he was fully insured,
And his Health-card shows he was once in hospital but left it cured.
Both Producers Research and High-Grade Living declare
He was fully sensible to the advantages of the Installment Plan
And had everything necessary to the Modern Plan,
A gramophone, a radio, a car and a frigidaire.
Our researchers into Public Opinion are content
That he held the proper opinions for the time of year;
When there was peace, he was for peace; when there was war, he went.
He was married and added five children to the population,
Which our Eugenist says was the right number for a parent of his generation,
And our teachers report that he never interfered with their education.
Was he free? Was he happy? The question is absurd:
Had anything been wrong, we should certainly have heard.

COMMENTARY

The biggest irony is that the unknown citizen is already dead at the start of the poem. Auden uses an inscription to prepare the reader's mind for a past tense account of an anonymous life remembered only by initials and a number. Another irony is that the reader would normally associate marble monuments and the word 'unknown' with dead soldiers, not dead citizens. Note though, toward the end:

'when there was war, he went'

Another satirical observation on education that still seems relevant today is that 'he never interfered with their education'. Notice again how the reader's normal expectation is contradicted: education should be for his benefit, not the teachers'. Note too the capitalisation of common nouns and noun phrases to give them emphasis (a literary convention of the 18th and 19th centuries revived): Greater Community, Union, Modern Man, Public Opinion.

Defining citizenship

Turn now from the discourse of poetic irony which has considerable power to call citizenship values into question and look at some modern definitions and word associations – back to lexicography again.

The *Longman New Universal Dictionary* (1982) defines a citizen in two ways:

1 an inhabitant of a city or town; esp. a freeman
2 a (native or naturalized) member of a state

Keith Faulks in *Citizenship In Modern Britain* (1998) gives a legal definition:

Citizenship is a status that denotes membership of a nation-state and which carries with it certain rights and duties associated with that citizenship.

In a formal definition of this kind one can sense power structures behind words like 'rights' and 'duties'.

In a letter to the authors, a representative from the Institute for Citizenship Studies quoted the Institute's Chief Executive, Jenny Talbot:

'The challenge lies in creating the conditions whereby all citizens feel able to become actively involved – can influence, persuade and campaign – and in the making of decisions can work together for the common good.'

This is more an attitude than a definition and certainly more dynamic than the notion of citizenship in the Auden poem. Notice how passively presented citizenship is in the poem, how frequently the descriptions of JS are indirect and evaluations of other people and organisations.

Another study of citizenship which you will find interesting is by E. Frazer and N. Lacy, *The Politics of Community* (1993). It argues that definitions of citizenship, which are apparently neutral, in fact reinforce gender inequality. Because of their traditional role as carers and child rearers, women are defined in terms of the civil community (ie private lives) and not in the political community (ie public lives). Their concerns are traditionally domestic rather than political. Jenny Talbot's concept includes women campaigners and also ethnic groups also shown by Frazer and Lacy to have been disadvantaged and excluded in matters of housing and education.

The notions of 'inclusion' and 'exclusion' are central components of the idea of citizenship. Insiders enjoy privileges, resources and rights. Outsiders, or those 'socially excluded' in modern jargon, enjoy none of these. In a British passport you will find the associated terms: 'exemption' and 'protection'.

ACTIVITY 47

Rights and responsibilities

You are going to begin an investigation of texts by first exploring semantic components of the word 'citizenship'. This is a bit like the lexicographical word webs you made earlier.

Four contrasts have been introduced: *rights* and *responsibilities* and *inclusion* and *exclusion.* The four don't match up neatly but there is some crossover. For example women have had a long history of *exclusion* from voting *rights.*

On a large sheet of paper, working with a partner, draw a vertical line down the middle. Put two headings, 'Rights' and 'Responsibilities' on either side of the line. Before analysing other people's views it will help if you sort out your own. Under the heading 'Rights' put all the things that citizenship entitles you to: for example, police, education, dole money. Do the same with 'Responsibilities', for example, safe driving, complying with hosepipe bans. You may find that some things, like voting, are both rights and responsibilities. You may also need to subdivide responsibilities into 'Liabilities' like paying taxes and 'Moral Duties' such as supporting a charity or 'keeping Britain tidy'.

Compare your ideas with those of other students. Do you detect ideological differences about rights and responsibilities. If so, decide where you stand.

Now do the same for 'Inclusion' and 'Exclusion'. You could start by looking at excluded persons and behaviours. Again, compare your ideas with those of other students and note ideological differences.

ACTIVITY 48

The Welfare State

With the coming of a new millennium and, in 1997, a change of government, it is not surprising that new ways of doing things and new ways of talking about things are in the air. There is evidence at this time that the British electorate were seeking a new set of civic values. The following series of texts are concerned with welfare. First, look at a feature of modern life established by a Conservative government, namely the Patients' Charter. You have already looked at a Social Care Charter in Chapter One.

Ask what role is assigned to the reader, what underlying assumptions it contains and identify the linguistic features that tell you these things.

Look especially at references to 'citizenship' and investigate what is meant by it.

TEXT 42

SALFORD F.H.S.A.

The Salford Family Health Services Authority is committed to working with its local family doctors to ensure that the services provided for you, the residents of Salford, are of the highest possible standard.

This leaflet has been produced by your doctor and the FHSA and sets out your rights as an NHS patient, the leaflet also explains the additional standards that your doctor and the practice staff are working towards achieving.

Although these rights and standards have been produced to further improve the quality of service available from your doctor, patients must also be aware of their responsibilities when using these services. These responsibilities are contained in this leaflet.

Our overall aim is to put the patient first, and we will be very pleased to hear from you with any comments you may have that will help us to improve the service provided. You will find our address on the back of this leaflet.

Did you know?
You Have These Rights.

- To be registered with a doctor.
- To change your doctor quickly and easily.

To be offered a health check:

- When joining a doctor's list for the first time.
- If you have not seen your doctor for three years.
- Every year, in your own home, if you are over 75.
- To receive emergency care at any time from a family doctor.
- To decide whether or not to see a trainee GP, to take part in medical research or medical student training.
- To be referred to a consultant, acceptable to you, for a first or second opinion when your GP considers it necessary.
- To be offered a clear explanation of any treatment you have been given.
- To have appropriate medicines prescribed for you as your GP thinks necessary.
- To have access to your doctor's practice leaflet giving information about the practice, the staff and services available at the surgery.
- To register with another doctor for contraceptive or maternity services if you are a woman.
- To see your medical records, subject to any limitations in the law and to know that your health records are confidential.
- To discuss with your doctor or Practice Manager any cause for concern.
- To receive a full and prompt reply to complaints you make about services.

Did you know?
That to achieve this
They need Your help.

- It is important that you understand any information you are given. If you are unsure about anything please **ask**.
- If you need a home visit, because you are housebound or too ill to come to the surgery.

Please-
Try to telephone before 10a.m.

- Understand that the receptionist may need to ask questions to help the doctor decide how urgent the visit is or if it is necessary.
- If you telephone to request an urgent surgery appointment.

Please:-

- Understand that the receptionist may need to ask questions to help the doctor decide how urgent the appointment is. Remember that all information given to practice staff is strictly confidential.

- Please do not call the doctor out unless it is an emergency that cannot wait until the next visit. Remember it may not necessarily be your own GP who visits you.
- Please try to be on time for your appointment, if you arrive late it may cause delays for other patients. If you need to cancel an appointment please contact the surgery as soon as possible.
- Please show courtesy and respect to your doctor and practice staff. There will be less of a chance of a misunderstanding if you are polite to each other.

Did you know?
Your Doctor and the Practice Staff are Working towards these Standards.

- To treat you as an individual and offer you courtesy and respect regardless of your **Ethnic origin, religion or Health problem.**
- To arrange, as appropriate, a home visit for patients who are too ill or infirm to come to the surgery.
- To keep waiting times for appointments to a minimum. When the doctor is unavoidably delayed eg: in an emergency you will be given an explanation after 30 minutes.
- To provide you with information about how to make suggestions or complaints about the care your doctor offers.
- To provide you with the names of the practice staff and to advise you on how to contact them.

COMMENTARY

Notice the recurring 'Did you know?' theme, an alternative to the familiar question/answer structure. This is a document with more accountability than a purely informative leaflet. Note too the words 'patients MUST also be aware of their responsibilities'. The twin rights/responsibilities element is acknowledged, coupled with the additional idea of 'standards'. Note also the strong semantic field created by such words as 'courtesy', 'respect', 'polite' and frequent uses of 'please'.

The discourse here contains many positives and its language puts the patient in a strong position. Note though a reservation voiced twice: 'as or when your GP considers it necessary'. This is a lessening of the rights and allows room for argument and interpretation. The slightly sceptical reader might also view the 'they need Your help' section as an opportunity to tackle recurring practice management problems. The notion 'Raising the Standard' should not be taken for granted either. It could mean standardising the existing quality of service or giving it the appearance of improvement. This is not an accusation of dishonesty but a recognition that the discourse wishes to create optimism and put the best face on problematical time.

ACTIVITY 49

What two governments said

The next two texts are examples of the same kind of discourse but were issued by two different governments. Both are about health and welfare.

The first text is part of the Conservative government's *Citizen's Charter* (1991). Note the singular form of 'Citizen'. Notice the title *Raising the Standard* echoed by the Conservative Local Authority, Salford, in the *Patient's Charter* you looked at previously.

Read the text and ask:

1 What role is assigned to the reader?
2 What assumptions underlie the text? How, for example, is citizenship presented?

As ever, to answer these questions you will need to look closely at lexical and grammatical choices and any other textual features.

TEXT 43 RAISING THE STANDARD

FOREWORD

I take great pleasure in the first set of initiatives under the Citizen's Charter. To make public services answer better to the wishes of their users, and to raise their quality overall, have been ambitions of mine ever since I was a local councillor in Lambeth over 20 years ago.

In the 1980s, reforms in schools, housing and hospitals gave people more say in how their services are run. Privatisation and contracting-out have transformed performance. The programme we are publishing today carries these reforms further – and into new territory. I want the Citizen's Charter to be one of the central themes of public life in the 1990s.

For this White Paper is only a beginning. Over the coming months, Ministers will be bringing forward more detailed plans for each service. But today we provide some early examples of how the principles of the Charter will be applied. How we will, for example, be introducing guaranteed maximum waiting times for hospital operations. How we will require all schools to provide parents with reports. How British Rail will be introducing new compensation schemes for poor service. How those who regulate electricity, water, gas and telecommunications will be given the same strong powers to insist on good service standards for the customer. How we will toughen up inspection and audit, relate pay more closely to performance, and provide the citizen with more and better information.

The Citizen's Charter is about giving more power to the citizen. But citizenship is about our responsibilities – as parents, for example, or as neighbours – as well as our entitlements. The Citizen's Charter is not a recipe for more state action; it is a testament of our belief in people's right to be informed and choose for themselves.

The White Paper sets out the mechanics for improving choice, quality, value and accountability. Not all apply to every service. But all have a common objective: to raise the standard of public services, up to and beyond the best at present available.

There is a well-spring of talent, energy, care and commitment in our public services. The aim of the Citizen's Charter is to release these qualities. Then we will have services in which the citizen can have confidence, and all public servants can have pride.

John Major

The range of mechanisms in the Charter covers:

- more privatisation;
- wider competition;
- further contracting-out;
- more performance-related pay;
- published performance targets – local and national;
- comprehensive publication of information on standards achieved;
- more effective complaints procedures;
- tougher and more independent inspectorates;
- better redress for the citizen when services go badly wrong.

THE PRINCIPLES OF PUBLIC SERVICE

Every citizen is entitled to expect:

■ Standards
Explicit standards, published and prominently displayed at the point of delivery. These standards should invariably include courtesy and helpfulness from staff, accuracy in accordance with statutory entitlements, and a commitment to prompt action, which might be expressed in terms of a target response or waiting time. If targets are to be stretched, it may not be possible to guarantee them in every case; minimum, as well as average, standards may be necessary. There should be a clear presumption that standards will be progressively improved as services become more efficient.

■ Openness
There should be no secrecy about how public services are run, how much they cost, who is in charge, and whether or not they are meeting their standards. Public servants should not be anonymous. Save only where there is a real threat to their safety, all those who deal directly with the public should wear name badges and give their name on the telephone and in letters.

■ Information
Full, accurate information should be readily available, in plain language, about what services are being provided. Targets should be published, together with full and audited information about

the results achieved. Wherever possible, information should be in comparable form, so that there is a pressure to emulate the best.

■ **Choice**
The public sector should provide choice wherever practicable. The people affected by services should be consulted. Their views about the services they use should be sought regularly and systematically to inform decisions about what services should be provided.

■ **Non-discrimination**
Services should be available regardless of race or sex. Leaflets are being printed in minority languages where there is a need. In Wales public bodies are aware of the needs of Welsh speakers.

■ **Accessibility**
Services should be run to suit the convenience of customers, not staff. This means flexible opening hours, and telephone inquiry points that direct callers quickly to someone who can help them.

■ **And if things go wrong?**
At the very least, the citizen is entitled to a good explanation, or an apology. He or she should be told **why** the train is late, or **why** the doctor could not keep the appointment. There should be a well-publicised and readily available complaints procedure. If there is a serious problem, it should be put right. And lessons must be learnt so that mistakes are not repeated. Nobody wants to see money diverted from service improvements into large-scale compensation for indifferent services. But the Government intends to introduce new forms of redress where these can be made to stimulate rather than distract from efficiency.

COMMENTARY

The discourse begins on a personal note and fluctuates between the first person singular and the first person plural. The 'citizen' is referred to twice in the singular and in the third person. The agents in this text are 'I/we' and 'they/those'. The Charter itself is described variously as a 'central theme' a 'testament' and most notably as something 'about giving power to the people'. What do you think 'about' means here? What difference would be made by saying the Charter 'will give power' or 'gives power'? Is it a matter of being deliberately vague? or of using brass-tacks language? If you look at the last sentence of the second paragraph ('one of the central themes of public life') the audience and reader role are clear. The document is addressed to providers; it is a policy directive. The Salford *Patient's Charter* is a response to that directive.

Characteristic of this kind of discourse is the use of words that belong to the common vocabulary but which have been given specialist meanings: mechanism, delivery, targets, explicit standards. Notice too relatively informal words used to signal that the government means business: tougher, go badly wrong.

One distinct difference between John Major's foreword and the 'mechanisms' and 'principles' page is the sustained use of modal verbs in the 'principles' section: may, must, should (especially should).

You are looking here at a White Paper designed to steer ways of thinking: it should not be surprising that its language is adopted in the process to show conformity. Notice though, the mixture of 'soft' words : courtesy, helpfulness, apology, openness; and 'hard' words to do with policy: privatisation, competition, contracted out, performance related pay, published performance targets.

ACTIVITY 50

Now look at a later government document, a Green Paper this time, *New Ambitions For Our Country: A New Contract for Welfare* (1998). It begins with a Foreword by the Prime Minister, this time Tony Blair. We have selected a page to follow this which is equivalent to the mechanisms and principles page of the Conservative party Charter.

Both documents have similar aims: to introduce powerful action by a government in aspects of social life that affect everybody. The effects of the 1991 Charter are already discernible in a variety of ways.

Set out below is a series of questions and suggestions to help you compare these texts in detailed ways.

1. Blair's Foreword is nearly three times longer than Major's. Summarise its content and explain what it is that has made one longer than the other.
2. What do you consider to be the main attitudes and guiding ideas in each document? Note key words that are different in each and decide if they are about different things or the same thing under a different name. For example, one document is called a 'Charter', the other a 'Contract'. What ideological difference does that suggest? Both are similar in their determination to be taken notice of: 'central themes of public life in the 1990s' and 'the beginning of a debate . . . up and down the country'.
3. Collect any words/phrases that seem to exemplify a difference of language/political style.
4. The 'Third Way' is sufficiently important for it to be signalled in the Foreword and detailed on the later page. Clearly this needs persuasive presentation; how is it presented? What does the contract actually mean?
5. Look at the eight key principles (bullet pointed) with the seven sub-headings on the principles page of the Charter.
6. Look especially at any civic references in the Contract: for example, citizen. How do you think 'citizens' are envisaged? Who are the 'us' and the 'we' at various points in both sections of the document?

TEXT 44

Foreword and Introduction From the Prime Minister

There has been no truly comprehensive review of the welfare state in all its elements since Beveridge. Individual benefits and contributions have been altered. But no one since then has attempted to survey the current system in its entirety, define its strengths and weaknesses and then lay out a political and intellectual framework for its reform and future development.

The result is not a blueprint for every benefit. This Green Paper marks the beginning of a debate, not its conclusion. We want it to be debated up and down the country, re-worked and refined, before we publish our proposals on the detail of the individual components of reform.

But the principles guiding reform and our vision of the future welfare state are clear. We want to rebuild the system around work and security. Work for those who can; security for those who cannot.

Substantial welfare reform is already happening. In the area of welfare to work, we have the New Deal, the largest assault on structural unemployment ever undertaken in this country, benefiting the young and long-term unemployed and, potentially, many lone parents, disabled people, and those with long-term illnesses. The Budget marked the first step in the transformation in how the tax and benefit system interacts with the world of work. The reform of student finance is the most important re-casting of the system for supporting our universities and students since higher education began to be extended beyond a small and privileged few. The radical alteration now proposed to our legal aid system, which will attempt to bring civil justice within the reach of ordinary citizens, is another.

For those of us who believe the welfare state is not just about cash benefits, but is about services too – like health and education – there are also hugely ambitious programmes of reform underway in our schools and hospitals.

Change can be controversial; and some of the ideas flagged up in this Green Paper will be too. Reform in areas such as pensions may stretch over decades, and is therefore a delicate political and administrative task. Our belief is that we should put in place a framework for reform, so that people can see the direction of reform and the shape of things to come. This will give confidence and security, enabling citizens and businesses to plan ahead. Reform is a vital part of rediscovering a true national purpose, part of a bigger picture in which our country is a model of the 21st century developed nation: with sound, stable economic management; dynamism and enterprise in business; the best educated and creative nation in the world; and a welfare state that promotes our aims and achievements.

We are acutely aware of the fears that even talk of welfare reform can arouse. For some, benefits are their lifeline. So we must approach reform sensitively and with the full engagement of the whole country.

But we should not forget why reform is right, and why, whatever the concerns over individual benefits, most people **know** it is right. Above all, the system must change because the world has changed, beyond the recognition of Beveridge's generation. The world of work has altered – people no longer expect a job for life; traditional industries have declined; new technologies have taken their place. There is a premium on skills and re-skilling throughout life. The role of women has been transformed. Family structures are different. We live longer, but work for fewer years. And the expectations of disabled people have changed out of all recognition, from half a century ago. We need a system designed not for yesterday, but for today.

But the welfare system has not kept pace with change. As a result, it is failing in its historical mission of creating a fairer and more prosperous society. There are three fundamental problems with the current system.

First, inequality has risen sharply and large numbers of people – particularly pensioners and children – are living in poverty. There are more homes of working age where no one works than would have been considered tolerable even 20 years ago. Yet the social security bill has risen far more than health or education. A system in which you spend more, but fail to stem urgent need, is plainly not working.

Secondly, the system all too often acts against those who want to work, creating a number of disincentives to move from benefits into the world of work. Disabled people, especially, face serious barriers to work.

Thirdly, the system urgently needs to reform because it is open to abuse. While many people do not get the benefits they are entitled to, others take advantage of the system. It is not just fraud, though that is unacceptably widespread, for example in Housing Benefit. The rules themselves can be bent as well as broken, rewarding those who play the system.

The question is often put: are these changes going to be 'cuts-driven' or 'reform driven'? The answer is clear: they are driven by the need to reform: but of course, in some reforming, we want to spend money in the fairest and most effective way. And in some cases, for example, for those severely disabled people with the greatest needs, or in our schools and hospitals, we will want to spend more. But in other cases, such as those who are socially excluded, we want to cut the cost of economic failure; not by lowering their standard of living but by raising their life chances. So we must have a system we can afford, but above all, we want a system that aids those who need it and helps people to help themselves.

We must return to first principles and ask what we want the welfare state to achieve. This is the question this Green Paper seeks to answer. In essence, it describes a third way: not dismantling welfare, leaving it simply as a low-grade safety net for the destitute; nor keeping it unreformed and underperforming; but reforming it on the basis of a new contract between citizen and state, where we keep a welfare state from which we all benefit, but on terms that are fair and clear.

There is a very simple reason why we need such a contract more than ever today. The welfare state we have is one from which the vast majority of us benefit through a state pension or Child Benefit or use of the NHS. The welfare state isn't just about a few benefits paid to the most needy.

But we all contribute through taxes and charges. We benefit but we pay. It is a contract between us as citizens. As such, it needs to be a fair deal, within a system that is clearer, more relevant for the modern world, efficiently run and where costs are manageable. One that is fair not just for the existing generation, but fair between the generations.

That is the fundamental reason for reform. It will take time. Frank Field has started the process in this Green Paper. Now that the process is underway, we want all the nation to be part of it. There will be consultation and time for discussion at every stage. Our objective is to build a genuine national consensus behind change. The welfare state belongs to us all. It is part of our inheritance. We must now all work together to re-build it for the new century that awaits.

Tony Blair

Prime Minister.

6 This third way will take us into the third stage of welfare. The welfare system will become pro-active, preventing poverty by ensuring that people have the right education, training and support. We will widen the exits from welfare dependency by offering tailor-made help for individuals.

7 Eight key principles will guide our reform programme:

- **The new welfare state should help and encourage people of working age to work where they are capable of doing so.**
- **The public and private sectors should work in partnership to ensure that, wherever possible, people are insured against foreseeable risks and make provisions for their retirement.**
- **The new welfare state should provide public services of high quality to the whole community, as well as cash benefits.**
- **Those who are disabled should get the support they need to lead a fulfilling life with dignity.**
- **The system should support families and children, as well as tackling the scourge of child poverty.**
- **There should be specific action to attack social exclusion and help those in poverty.**
- **The system should encourage openness and honesty and the gateways to benefit should be clear and enforceable.**
- **The system of delivering modern welfare should be flexible, efficient and easy for people to use.**

Corporate citizenship

An irony of both the *Trainspotting* excerpt and the Auden poem is that the worthwhileness of existence is expressed in terms of consumer goods possessed: 'big television … washing machines, cars, compact disc players and electrical tin openers' in the one, and 'A gramophone, a radio, a car and a frigidaire' in the other.

Note that Auden maintains a focus on one individual throughout the poem, his possessions all in the singular. In the *Trainspotting* excerpt, the 'big television' is singular, all the other items are pluralised. Auden's poem, though satirical, is moving because of the individual focus; the *Trainspotting* excerpt makes its point very effectively but because it is a general attack, the reader can easily exclude himself from the people being satirised.

In addition to commodities and consumption, Auden's poem is about political forces that control people's lives. The 'unknown citizen' is himself a commodity in the system, living an anonymous life that nevertheless conforms to the statistical expectations and requirements of government. His vote, the most obvious political power possessed by a commodity, can be controlled by persuading his opinions.

The next series of texts you are going to look at are about modern ethical business practices. Pressure groups over the last twenty or thirty years have forced both governments and businesses to face their moral and social responsibilities as corporate citizens. Sociologists have also drawn attention to ways in which large business organisations, especially global ones, exercise more control over people's lives than government itself.

Before turning to the texts, it will help to look at some of the language used by sociologists and economists when discussing business power and ethical implications. You will need to understand these terms (their discourse) in order to understand the contexts and ideologies in which the texts are produced and interpreted.

In *A New View Of Society*, Robert Owen (1771–1858) asked himself this question: 'What are the best arrangements under which these men and their families can be well and economically lodged, fed, clothed, trained, educated, employed and governed?' Owen's writing and actions marked the beginning of the philanthropic movement in which some industrialists and business organisations exercised some of their power (and profits) for the benefit of the wider society.

The perceived inequality of power and influence between capital and labour, producer and consumer, nevertheless continued and strengthened in the 20th century, regardless of individual acts of philanthropy such as endowing schools, libraries and art galleries; creating public parks; funding hospitals. There are two famous contrary statements of the modern situation, both by distinguished American economists. Neither sees Owenism or philanthropy as the natural state of affairs but more of a charity.

J. K. Galbraith, in *American Capitalism* (1956) described the relationship between big business, its employees and customers as follows:

'Private economic power is held in check by the countervailing power of those who are subject to it.'

If you look at Jenny Talbot's description of citizenship you will get a 1990s idea of what 'countervailing power' means. The term also applies to labour unions and consumer groups.

Milton Friedman in *Capitalism and Freedom* (1982) offers a hard-nosed description:

'There is only one responsibility of business – to use its resources to engage in activities to increase its profits so long as it stays within the rules of the game, engages in open and free competition, without deception or fraud.'

Much has happened since the 1950s and 1960s. However accurate Friedman may be in his description of a prevailing business attitude, the growing influence of countervailing forces shows how profoundly unsatisfactory large sections of society find Friedman's view.

People are not just consumers/customers; citizenship is more than getting and spending, more than the life of JS in Auden's poem.

Thus by the 1990s we have arrived at a concept of 'corporate citizenship'.

In his *Corporate Citizenship* (1996), Chris Marsden defines corporate citizenship as follows:

'A good corporate citizen might be identified by its openly communicated contribution to the economy, ethical business practices, good human resource management, environmental responsibility and community and public affairs involvement, benchmarked against agreed good practice.'

In *The Search for Corporate Citizenship*, Michael Clark, Professor of Public Policy, wrote:

'The search for a better understanding of corporate citizenship is on!... The reader will be struck by the variety of meaning ...'.

In Galbraith's terms it could mean responding to countervailing forces; in Friedman's, it could mean furthering business self-interest more subtly.

Corporate citizenship is balanced against personal citizenship. There has been a rising tide of communication from corporate citizen addressed to ordinary citizens (you and us) with the express purpose of reassuring customers of how ethical a company's business practices are.

ACTIVITY 51

Corporate responsibility

Below is the text of a worksheet used by Dunelm Management Consultancy as a prompt for discussion groups on a junior management training course. It summarises five principles of good corporate citizenship as set out by Marsden and Andriof in *Towards An Understanding of Corporate Citizenship and How to Influence It* (1998).

Read it as a preparation for exploring texts concerned especially with ethical business. As a longer term activity you could use it as a start in collecting leaflets, articles and advertisements by firms drawing attention to their efforts in the five areas of good corporate citizenship.

TEXT 45

For Marsden and Andriof good corporate citizenship means:

- contributing to the economy: by generating wealth through jobs and profits. Profits are maximised by balancing quality with value-for-money
- demonstrating environmental responsibility: by prioritising sustainable development, reducing emissions, using energy efficiently, improving a product's life-cycle and controlling waste
- getting involved in the wider community: by supporting cultural activities, investing in education programmes, regenerating the inner city and doing volunteer work
- practising ethical business (exercising moral standards through fair trade): by observing human rights (not mistreating indigenous people, for example, through child labour), observing advertising standards, not producing anti-social products, paying bills on time, not offering bribes and telling the truth
- managing human resources with integrity: by implementing equal opportunities in staff recruitment and retention, training staff, balancing work with home and managing redundancy

ACTIVITY 52

Corporate profiles

An emphasis on scrutiny, audit and accountability are very much a part of economic ideology and discourse in the 1990s. The *Which* Report philosophy of the 1960s, then concerned chiefly with consumer goods such as those listed in the Auden poem and the *Trainspotting* excerpt, has extended now to what *The Times* refers to as 'Corporate Profiles' in which the paper puts a whole business organisation under the microscope.

Below are some excerpts from their profile of Abbey National. Read them noting the mixture of formal economics language and less formal expressions that typify this kind of 'expert, investigative journalism'. What attitudes are conveyed in the discourse by the occasional use of informal and figurative language.

TEXT 46

CORPORATE PROFILE: *Abbey National*

IF YOU live in a 1930s London house, the chances are that its construction was financed by Abbey National. The former building society, then known simply as Abbey Road after the location of its headquarters, helped to build the city's suburbs by pioneering an innovative lending scheme. The proceeds ultimately allowed it to outgrow its own London roots and later to merge with the National Building Society.

Being in the vanguard is a habit that Abbey finds difficult to let go. It was the first building society to test the waters of the stock market, converting to a bank in 1989. Remarkably, for a long while it managed to retain the cuddly, safe image associated with mutual lenders, while behaving much like any other high street bank.

Throughout Abbey's history, mortgage lending has been at the heart of its business. On the basis of outstanding loans, it is the country's second-biggest lender, with a 14 per cent market share. Only Halifax – now also a bank – is larger, providing one in five of the nation's home loans. But all is not well at Abbey's core.

Its share of net new lending has plunged in recent years, reaching its nadir in the first quarter of 1997 when new loans hit zero. New entrants to the market have been able to undercut the traditional players with their expensive branch networks. Simultaneously, the remaining mutuals, led by Nationwide, have embarked on a discounting campaign. On top of that, the Great British mortgage is fast becoming a commodity item.

"There is no long-term future in the mortgage market," admits Ian Harley, the former Abbey finance director who took over the job of chief executive earlier this year. "The market is growing at just 5 per cent per year." He said recently that Abbey's share of new loans was unlikely to exceed 5 per cent in 1998.

WHAT THE EXPERTS SAY

"The gloss is wearing off Abbey National. The brand doesn't carry as much weight as perhaps four or five years ago, and it could do with picking up a dedicated life brand such as Norwich Union or Legal & General. But prices are too high at the moment. Otherwise, with a 5 per cent decline in spreads on mortgage business, we see net income coming down in the first half." – *Rob Down, ABN Amro.*

"It's really steady-as-she-goes at Abbey National. Strategically, an acquisition would make sense: it has both the capital and experience to do that. But Abbey also needs to do some hard strategic thinking about how it jazzes up the mortgage business. The market is growing at about 6 per cent per annum. You would hope to keep up with that or you do have a worry." – *John Leonard, Salomon Smith Barney.*

OUR VERDICT

Ethical expression[1]	3/10
Fat-cat quotient[2]	9/10
Financial Record	7/10
Share performance	9/10
Attitude to employees	8/10
Strength of brand	7/10
Innovation	4/10
Annual report	6/10
City star rating	7/10
Future prospects	5/10
Total	
65/100	

Ethical expression is evaluated by [1]*Integrity Works.* The Fat-cat quotient, in which best boardroom pay practice scores highest, is provided by [2]*Crisp Consulting*

THE FACTS

Pre-tax profits (1997): £1.4bn before exceptionals
Total assets: £150.8bn
Market cap: £15.2bn
Proportion of profit from non-traditional activities: 49.3 per cent
Share of the UK mortgage market: 14 per cent
Employees: 25,464
Overview: Has diversified away from savings and mortgages to embrace treasury operations, life insurance, pensions and general insurance

The Times, 25 May 1998

COMMENTARY

Note phrases such as 'the gloss is wearing off', 'carry as much weight', 'steady-as-she goes', 'jazzes up', 'fat cats', 'cuddly safe image', 'runs a tight ship'.

Note too, the sentence: 'The Great British mortgage is fast becoming a commodity item' and the term 'ethical expression' in the Our Verdict table (see also the footnote, 'Integrity Works').

Notice that there are two linguistic influences at work here. There are the everyday terms that are very accessible, memorable evaluations of aspects of the company. There is also the use of a word like 'commodity' which belongs to the discourse of economics. Its use here signals a significant change in the way that mortgages are coming to be regarded.

ACTIVITY 53

An investigation

In order to understand discourse in action it is helpful to look at a case study: the nature of discourse is not always easy to appreciate in excerpts from de-contextualised texts.

One very significant countervailing force to emerge in modern society is Greenpeace. When it was learned that the petroleum giant Shell intended dumping its redundant floating oil store in the Atlantic, Greenpeace successfully challenged the company. This and other negative publicity campaigns reduced sales, lowered staff morale and triggered Shell to reconsider its environmental responsibilities:

'We believe we acted honourably ... But that is not enough. Clearly, the conviction that you are doing things right is not the same as getting them right. For us it has been a salutary lesson.'

In *The Times* (23 April, 1998), Graham Sergeant wrote an account of the whole matter, *Shell Puts Itself in for the Hamburger Test.* As a consequence, Shell published a publicity statement, *Profits and Principles: Does There Have to be a Choice?*, in which it sets out a long term strategy to better integrate and audit its environmental and economic policies. The Business Ethics Network (UK) also contributed to the debate: 'nobody's perfect, and if we don't get it 100% right, we'll be all over the papers'.

Read the article in *The Times* (on CD-Rom or in a Reference Library archive) and read the two leaflets by sending for them or using the Internet. You may also find other documents on the Internet. With these texts you will be able to investigate the discourse of public argument about an ethical business issue.

Certainly there is material here for a project or it may lead you to collect texts on another issue that interests you.

Ethical trading

We turn now to a series of texts in which companies advertise their ethical awareness and policies. Reputation enhancement is quite clearly a general motive but look closely at attitudes and beliefs encoded in the adverts and at the kind of responses hoped for from readers. Remember that reader response isn't just a matter of liking/not liking; it is also a matter of recognition of something that interests you or of which you approve but which may not be the product itself.

ACTIVITY 54

Washing machines

Look at transcript of the advertisement below and identify which of the Marsden and Andriof corporate citizen messages are encoded here (to remind yourself what they are, see page 99). The advert appeared in the *Radio Times*, August 1997. Identify any other issues that interest you.

TEXT 47

Water

"What's so special about the way it uses water?" He said.

Now, if you're like me, you'll realise that the simple things in life are often men. "We all know clothes are washed using water, right? Well, Candy has looked at how water can wash clothes better," I explained. "Candy?" he mumbled.

It all made perfect sense to me, but I could see my new Candy Activa needed explaining further.

"Yes. They've invented a system that shoots a high powered jet of clean water through the wash as it spins, while another cleans the detergent drawer to make sure all the powder is used." He still looked doubtful.

"And they've found a way of doing all this while using 30% less water. Brilliant, eh?"

"But why didn't you ask me for advice, first." He reproached.

"Because," I said as sweetly as I could, "I've chosen. It's Candy."

COMMENTARY

In Marsden/Andriof terms, the advert has made the conservation of water a priority issue. It doesn't waste water; it uses 30% less water, but less than what or whom is not stated. It doesn't waste detergent either. But notice that saving water is only the third selling point. The ordering of things has important stylistic consequences. What then are the selling points thought to be stronger?

1 that by buying the product, a woman will assert her independence
2 the quality of the product.

Certainly this argument nods in the direction of the first Marsden/Andriof indicator (value-for-money products).

The advertisement also contains very strong gender signals. Where do these fit into the Marsden/Andriof list, if at all? There is much common sense in showing a strong gender bias in an advert designed for the people who make the choice of which machine to buy, so there is not necessarily a feminist edge here. Indeed, many modern women would disapprove at the gratuitous insults and the aggressive finale to the advert because it stereotypes supposed feminist attitudes.

Another message is that women can understand technology without help from men.

ACTIVITY 55

The most honest cosmetic company in the world

Compared with other global companies, The Body Shop has a remarkable reputation. Below are three texts produced by The Body Shop. The first advertises a face cleansing gel (note 'cleansing' not 'cleaning'; what nuance of meaning do you detect in the use of the word 'cleansing' by cosmetic firms as opposed to the word 'cleaning'? Do the two words belong to different semantic fields even though they have the same basic meaning (ie to get dirt off?) The second is a campaign statement as part of their cosmetics advertising, the third – well, you decide what kind of discourse it is.

List the indicators of corporate citizenship in the campaign statement. Do you see any conflict between the campaign statement and the advert for a face cleansing gel. How effectively have you been educated by the publicity?

TEXT 48

Have you ever realised how often *face* is used in everyday language? We're told to *put on a brave face* and *face the music*; we hear about *the changing face* of fashion and *in your face* attitudes. The reason? Our face tells our life's story. It shows the world who we are, what we're thinking, what mood we're in, our state of health and in some places (with the help of a few tribal tattoos), even wards off evil spirits.

All that puts a big strain on the face. It needs looking after. This booklet highlights just some of the products from The Body Shop you can use to keep your face looking healthy and feeling good.

We don't promise a cure for wrinkles (nor is one needed!) We don't offer ways to make you look younger. What we do and always have done, is sell products that care for your skin and hair and in doing so, care for you.

YOU'VE DONE IT!

The Government has announced that the testing of finished cosmetic products on animals will be banned immediately and tests on cosmetic ingredients reviewed.
Thousands of animals will be saved from suffering in the future because you have joined The Body Shop and other campaigning organisations to stand up against what you believe is a cruel and unnecessary practice.
Well done! but it ain't over yet . . .

WHAT NEXT?

WE WILL WORK WITH THE GOVERNMENT TO ENSURE INGREDIENT TESTS ARE BANNED. SOON, WE'LL BE ASKING YOU TO JOIN WITH US ONCE MORE. WE WANT OUR GOVERNMENT TO CHAMPION A TOTAL BAN ON ANIMAL TESTING OF COSMETICS IN THE EUROPEAN UNION, TO SAVE MANY MORE THOUSANDS OF ANIMALS.

So, it's thanks to the Government for taking a great first step on animal testing in the cosmetics industry. But, most of all, it's thanks to you, our campaigning customers, for showing how individual customer power can make a real difference. Fantastic!

THANK YOU!

THE BODY SHOP

lived and loved
life: how we've raised kids; enjoyed
good meals, a drink and a laugh; suffered,
shrugged and moved on. That has to change.
I've been saying so for nearly two decades.
But I just don't see that change coming. In
fact, the pressure on women to conform to
a physical ideal is, if anything, getting worse.
So I want to start a revolution in thinking.
Our targets are sexism, size-ism and age-ism.
Our weapon is self-esteem. I'm not sure we fully
appreciate how fundamental self esteem is. As the
root of dignity and personal freedom, it is also
the cornerstone of political activism and democracy.
It makes sense – the way we feel about ourselves
is going to have a huge impact on the way we feel
about our world. So it really is time for change.
The revolution starts here.
Anita Roddick

COMMENTARY

The Body Shop has long been aware of the power of both body and verbal language. It is still unusual to get a knowledgeable and imaginative mini-lecture in linguistics as an opener to a cosmetics advertisement.

The 'You've done it' leaflet advertises that Body Shop campaigns are a power for change. Note that the second person is used several times but it is not clear who is congratulating whom until the end when both government legislation and 'individual customer power' are explicitly congratulated and thanked by The Body Shop. Quite a remarkable self confidence, but then the corporate citizenship shown by this company in the 1980s proved very significant in raising awareness and materially supporting Greenpeace to 'Save The Whale' and Friends of the Earth in its campaigns against acid rain and in support of recycling.

Before turning to the next activity look at the text below taken from *Marie Claire* (August 1998). In an earlier activity it was noted that *Marie Claire* was illustrated with exploited, vulnerable images of women and that there was ambiguity in the combination of text and pictures. The editorial below allies itself quite unreservedly with Body Shop and lists its own achievements in the support of human rights.

TEXT 49

Insiders' guide

marie claire

Welcome to this special August

issue of *Marie Claire*, which focuses on body image and self-esteem – two subjects that we know are close to our readers' hearts. Inside, Geri Halliwell reveals exclusively in her own words, why she's happy with her shape and how it feels to be under constant media scrutiny. Discussion about body shapes and sizes is guaranteed to provoke controversy – not something we have ever shied away from. Over the years, *Marie Claire* has explored these issues in a series of ground-breaking articles. As long ago as 1990, we asked readers to pose naked and tell us what they love about their shapes, for 'In Celebration Of the Female Body'. In December 1995 we talked to men about why they prefer larger women as sexual partners; then, last year, we asked if the sexes think alike when it comes to the perfect body shape.

This month, *Marie Claire* and The Body Shop are working together to develop awareness of stereotyping about weight and size. The Body Shop has come up with some dramatic statistics. For example, 75 per cent of us diet, but 95 per cent of diets don't work; 90 per cent of women want to lose weight, but only sixteen per cent are obese. So, what's the point of it all? It's simple. We are endorsing our long-established philosophy that size and shape don't matter; being happy and healthy is what it's all about.

So, while The Body Shop launches its voluptuous Ruby doll – as an alternative to the usual svelte 'role models' – along with *Full Voice* magazine, which is dedicated to body-shape issues, our Reportage this month explores 'Your Body Through The Ages'. We asked four groups of women, whose bodies are their livelihoods, how they feel about the struggle to maintain peak physical condition. Plus, we talk to a mother and daughter who have both suffered from anorexia. Then, in a special Voyeur page, Anita Roddick reveals her commitment to promoting women's self-esteem. Finally, we have a special gift – an Aromatherapy Refreshing Bergamot Body Spritzer from The Body Shop, worth £8.95 – for every reader.

We hope you find this issue as illuminating and challenging as we did when we were putting it together.

Juliet Warkentin, Editor

ACTIVITY 56

Your money and your life

This text was published by the Co-operative Bank in their customers' newsletter, *In Touch* (1997). Read it and decide what kind of discourse is going on. What is the author doing? What role is assigned to the reader? What is the ideology behind it? Identify ways in which information, instruction and persuasion are mixed.

We have abbreviated the text to make it manageable. The 'seven key partners' section contains just the headings.

Summarise the argument, which is an interesting one in itself, and identify the cultural references, for example to the Celtic world.

TEXT 50

Strength

TERRY THOMAS

The Seven Partners Concept
DEVELOPED FROM THE WRITINGS AND SUCCESSFUL ACTIVITIES OF ROBERT OWEN 1771–1858

Many commentators have said that stakeholding is a threat to enhancing shareholder value. They then get lost in a dogmatic argument as to what stakeholding actually is or is not.

We need a long-term blueprint to allow business to prosper. My life-long experience as a banker tells me that a combination of the Anglo-Saxon capitalist model with Robert Owen's inclusive approach to a company's key partners, provides this. These partners include all groups who are directly or indirectly affected by a company's activities.

A spirit of co-operation between natural partners within an organisation (see diagram) is essential to any enterprise. It is important to place this spirit in context. The 18th and 19th centuries brought forth Adam Smith, one of the founders of Capitalism; Karl Marx, regarded as the founder of Communism; and Robert Owen, who is credited as the founder of Co-operation, at least within the Anglo-Saxon and Celtic worlds.

The experiment of communism has failed. Equally, all democratic countries, whilst advertising capitalism, have passed laws and continue to do so, to safeguard citizens from the excesses of capitalism.

Looking towards the 21st Century, it appears to me as a banker and a businessman that the marketplace is being driven by consumers towards the need for co-operation. Most particularly, co-operation as partners within an enterprise.

Robert Owen's middle view, between Smith on the right and Marx on the left, has prevailed. It will continue to succeed.

Since my school days I have been inspired by the writings of Robert Owen, a fellow Welshman, who was born in Newtown in 1771 and died there in 1858. His writings reveal him as a man ahead of his time; an industrialist and social reformer, who came to be regarded as the founder of the Co-operative movement.

Robert Owen's experimentation, apart from his unsuccessful co-operative community of New Harmony in Indiana, was entirely within corporate organisations. He was a successful industrialist who demonstrated at the textiles mill, New Lanark, that by caring for your internal partners you could increase your profits and enhance shareholder value.

Robert Owen's business model is explained in his essays, A New View of Society. It combines the rigour and discipline of the marketplace with a focus on nurturing co-operative relationships with the company's natural partners. The model sets out a long-term view for managing the financial aspects of a business to ensure continued success.

Robert Owen's values can be used by any company to define how it can co-operate effectively with those partners crucial to its success.

GIVE AND TAKE

This is the basis of the challenging renewed business model. At the heart of the approach to this model is the single phrase – 'to treat every partner in balance and across time'. Each arrow on the partnership chart points in both directions indicating mutual dependence. We depend upon our partners and they depend upon us. There must always be give and take. And every right must be balanced with responsibility. That is the spirit of co-operation.

I believe that the Anglo-Saxon view of capitalism does eventually and inevitably lead to short-termism in decision-making because of overwhelming pressure on managers for short-term results. Whereas the 'Rhine' model, initially the more successful of the two capitalistic models, so protects itself from the rigours of the market place that it eventually becomes inefficient, incestuous and even corrupt.

Robert Owen's middle way, so ridiculed by Marx and Engels as 'Utopian', has in fact proved the

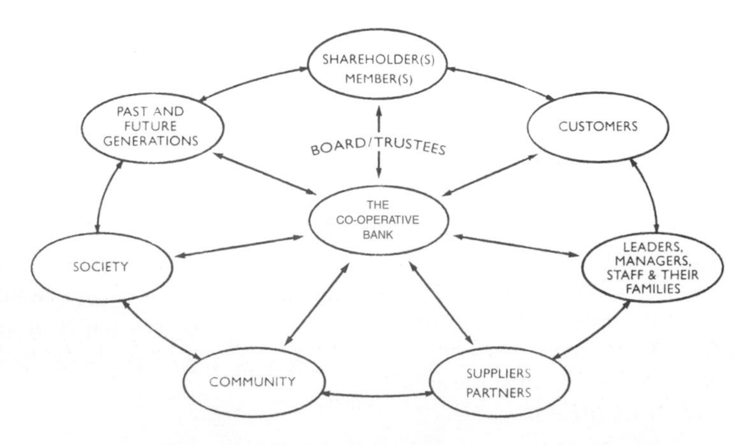

most successful formula. I suggest that the combination of the Anglo-Saxon approach to competition, with Robert Owen's spirit of co-operation through an inclusive partnership, is the way forward into the 21st Century. In fact 'Tomorrow's Company', or 'Tomorrow's Co-operative'.

COMMENTARY

Clearly the author believes in persuasion by information and teaching. The article is almost a seminar on economics for beginners. We advise you to acquire a copy of the complete text from the bank, or look on the Internet. One theme of modern socio-economic thought is inclusivity as opposed to exclusivity. Here, an inclusive model is advocated. Note too that there is a strong tone of moral intention toward the end.

ACTIVITY 57

Every little bit counts

The texts below contrast the approaches of two well known Supermarkets to ethical business: Tesco and Somerfield. Text 51 describes Somerfield's commitment to community charities. Text 52 describes Tesco's nominated charity of the year. These campaigns are in addition to such activities as eliminating animal testing and donating computers to schools.

Read the texts and decide what indicators of corporate citizenship are being signalled. What do they have in common as far as discourse is concerned? Are there any significant differences in style and approach to charity?

TEXT 51

ONE OF THESE CHILDREN WOULD LIKE TO RUN AS FAST AS THE OTHERS.
A BONE MARROW TRANSPLANT WILL BE A STEP IN THE RIGHT DIRECTION.

HELPING YOUR CHOICE OF LOCAL GOOD CAUSES

NOW, FROM YOUR COMMUNITY STORE, YOUR COMMUNITY CHARITY!

Each year Somerfield and their customers raise thousands of pounds for their local communities. Now we hope that literally millions of pounds will be raised through the new Somerfield Community Charity.

The Somerfield Community Charity is a really effective way to help your local community, as you nominate the local good causes which you think are the most deserving.

There is a dedicated Somerfield Community Charity notice board in every Somerfield store, so you can see how your local community benefits, and how you can participate.

OUR PLEDGE: NOT ONE PENNY PROFIT TO SOMERFIELD BUT MILLIONS OF POUNDS TO GOOD CAUSES*

The Somerfield Community Charity is a non-profit making organisation which has been established with the specific objective of raising money to support local community based good causes in the area surrounding each Somerfield store.

It is intended that 80% of the proceeds raised for the Somerfield Community Charity will be donated to local good causes nominated by the customers of each store.

*Depending on funds raised for Somerfield Community Charity

SOME OF THE LOCAL GOOD CAUSES ALREADY SUGGESTED

We asked Somerfield customers where they would like to see the money raised being donated – here are just a few of their suggestions:
EQUIPMENT FOR THE LOCAL SCHOOL
Computers, Sports Equipment, Musical Instruments
URGENTLY NEEDED REPAIRS
for the local Church or Scout Hut
MEDICAL EQUIPMENT FOR THE LOCAL HOSPITAL
Contribute towards the cost of a scanner or incubators
TRANSPORT FOR THE DISABLED
Contribute to the running costs of specially adapted transport
HELP SAVE CRITICALLY ILL CHILDREN
Fund sending them abroad for a vital operation

OUR COMMITMENT TO THE NSPCC

The remaining 20% of proceeds raised for the Somerfield Community Charity will, in 1997, be donated to the NSPCC, Britain's leading charity specialising in child protection and the prevention of cruelty to children.

Since it was founded in 1884, millions of children have benefited from the work of the NSPCC, which delivers its service through over 120 local Teams and Projects and the National Child Protection Helpline (0800 800 500), a 24 hour freephone service which answers on average 1200 calls a week from people concerned about children.

VOTE FOR YOUR LOCAL GOOD CAUSE NOW

The Somerfield Community Charity is a really effective way to help your local community, as you nominate the local good causes which you think are the most deserving.

With your help we can make a real difference in your local area.

You can nominate the local good cause you feel is most deserving by completing a nomination card and posting it in the box on the notice board in every Somerfield store.* Alternatively, if there are no nomination cards available plain paper entries will be acceptable. (Only one nomination per customer per nomination period.)

The good cause receiving the most votes every nomination period could be the beneficiary of the store's fundraising activity.

FROM APRIL 7th YOU CAN GIVE TO CHARITY AND WIN UP TO £50,000

*Excluding Somerfield Staines Store

TEXT 52

Introducing our 1997 Charity of the Year

What is the Tesco Charity of the Year Scheme?

As part of our continued commitment to support our local communities, each year we adopt a charity to be the main focus for our staff fund-raising activities. The Tesco Charity of the Year for 1997 is Mencap (Enable in Scotland) and our staff up and down the country will be taking part in events and activities to raise funds for Mencap's Blue Sky Appeal.

As with all our staff fund-raising, funds raised for Mencap's Blue Sky Appeal will be topped up by 20% from the Tesco Charity Trust.

Previous Tesco charities of the year have included the Muscular Dystrophy Group, Riding for the Disabled Association, Save the Children and the NSPCC. Each one of these charities has had its funds significantly increased as a result of Tesco staff fund-raising – in some instances by more than £1 million.

If you would like to help with our fund-raising efforts, look out for competitions, activities or events organised by staff in your local Tesco store.

What does Mencap do?

Over the last 50 years, Mencap has cared, campaigned and supported people with a learning disability by providing education and training, independent homes, advice and friendship, employment and leisure opportunities as well as pioneering new ways of caring.

What is a Learning Disability?

Learning disability (formerly known as mental handicap) is the most common form of disability in Britain, affecting around 1.2 million people. It is caused by damage to a person's brain before or after birth or by genetic factors like Downs Syndrome or autism. It is a life long condition resulting in difficulty in learning, behavioural problems and other social disadvantages. While the range of disabilities is enormous – great things can be achieved with the right support and advice.

How will the money raised by Tesco staff fund-raising be spent?

Looking ahead to the next 50 years, Mencap has launched the Blue Sky Appeal. Money raised by Tesco staff will contribute locally to the Blue Sky Appeal and enable Mencap to put in place a new and national network of Family Advisers. This service will provide a network of accessible, high quality family and personal support services in every part of the UK to people with learning disabilities and their families (in Scotland, this will be done through Mencap's sister organisation, known as Enable).

If you:

- **would like to become involved in local Mencap activities**
- **could support a fund-raising event**
- **would like more information about Mencap and the Blue Sky Appeal**
- **would like to make a contribution to Mencap**

Please write for an information pack to:
Tesco Charity of the Year 1997
Mencap Blue Sky Appeal
Freepost
London EC1B 1AA
or call 0645 777 779
You don't need to use a stamp, but it will save the charity money if you do. Cheques can be made payable to **Mencap, Blue Sky Appeal**
Donations by cheque can also be made through your local Tesco store. Please ask a member of staff for details.

COMMENTARY

There is a difference in style between the two supermarkets. Somerfield uses the word 'community' several times and invites customers to nominate charities they would like to see supported. In effect they are acting as a channel for, or an agent of, their customers' wishes. The power to decide has been given to the customers/fellow citizens. Certainly the community aspect of the Marsden/Andriof indicators is seen as an important part of corporate citizenship. Note the use of we/you pronouns indicating joint agency. Tesco on the other hand may be thought of as paternalistic in that they have themselves decided which charity will be supported. Note the use of predominantly we/our pronouns. 'You' is largely reserved for requesting information rather than for acting. The term 'Charity of the Year' which might be thought of as an accolade for Tesco does in fact refer to Tesco's choice of charity for 1997.

ACTIVITY 58

Church militant

The practice of 'naming and shaming' is something citizens have come to expect from government in recent years. Bureaucratic inefficiencies, run down schools, hospital waiting lists have all come under government scrutiny, been found wanting and been publicly named and shamed. But government departments are not the only watchdogs. The organisation, Christian Aid has a pretty formidable record for aggressive scrutiny and for saying what it thinks.

Below is the text of a leaflet on the ethical progress made by supermarkets. Read it and ask: what role does it assign to the reader? What ideology lies behind it? What features of language are significant?

TEXT 53

Supermarkets' ethical progress

Christian Aid is campaigning for British supermarkets to give workers in developing countries a fairer deal.

At present many have to endure harsh conditions and ill treatment to produce the goods that are sold on our supermarket shelves.

Some supermarkets are responding really well to the campaign, others not so well. The table ranks each chain according to its response to Christian Aid's campaign – calling for all supermarkets to adopt independently monitored codes of conduct guaranteeing minimum working conditions for their own brand suppliers.

We are not asking you to change your supermarket. We are asking supermarkets to change. Please check their progress against the list below.

Position	Supermarket
1	Tesco
2	Safeway
2	Sainsbury
4	Co-op (CWS)
5	Asda
6	Waitrose
7	Kwik Save
8	Somerfield
9	Morrisons
10	Marks & Spencer

Oct 97

For more information ring Christian Aid on 0171–523 2264.

Christian Aid
We believe in life before death

COMMENTARY

The first thing you are likely to notice is that in the leaflet (contemporary with the two supermarket texts in the last activity) Tesco rates number one and Somerfield, number eight. As it says at the bottom, if you want more information on how these ratings are arrived at you will have to contact Christian Aid. The text beside the ratings is mainly informational but note the flair for catchphrases in the campaign: 'We are not asking you to change your supermarket. We are asking supermarkets to change'. See also, 'We believe in life before death'. The text on the back of the leaflet is considerably more aggressive. It asks for help politely at the outset but, in a series of imperatives asks you to join the campaign and take direct personal action, even to the extent of pinning the notice up in supermarkets (a real test of how genuinely controlled by customers, the notice board is). You are also asked to discuss it with the manager. The government promise to get tough with unsatisfactory public services is catching on.

ACTIVITY 59

Baby Milk Action versus Nestlé

Below are texts of a controversy between a global business organisation and a pressure group. The Baby Milk Action leaflet featured a cartoon captioned: 'Don't be a mug. Give Nescafe the boot'. Nestlé is the parent company of Nescafe. On the reverse of the leaflet are arguments against Nestlé and a call to boycott their goods. The leaflet is followed by a Nestlé bulletin taken from the Internet and dated 14 April, 1998.

Read both texts and note the language and textual strategies used by the two parties. You will not be able to decide on the facts of the matter because of a lack of independent evidence. Concentrate on the features of discourse which will reveal attitudes.

TEXT 54

A baby dies every 30 seconds from unsafe bottle feeding

■ **Nestlé** aggressively promote their baby milks to mothers and health workers to ensure that infants are bottle fed. Such promotion is condemned by UNICEF and WHO.

■ If babies are given bottles, they are less able to suckle well. This makes breastfeeding failure more likely.

■ The water mixed with baby milk powder in poor conditions is often unsafe. This leads to diarrhoea and often death. *Each day, 400 babies die from unsafe bottle feeding, says* UNICEF.

■ Baby milk is very expensive: it can cost over 50% of the family income.

■ Poor people often have to over-dilute the baby milk powder to make it last longer. The baby is then likely to become malnourished.

■ Breastfeeding is free, safe and protects against infection. Even undernourished mothers can breastfeed.

■ **But Nestlé know that if they don't get babies on the bottle, they don't do business.**

Don't let them get away with it – Boycott Nescafé.

TEXT 55

Q What was the controversy on infant formula about?

A

A boycott was launched in 1977 against Nestlé and our products by activists in the United States who were concerned at the marketing practices of infant formula by the industry in the Developing World. This lead to the adoption in 1981 by the World Health Assembly of the World Health Organization of the International Code of Marketing of Breast-milk Substitutes. This stated that there was a 'legitimate market' for infant formula. The aim of the Code is to ensure safe and adequate nutrition, not only through the protection and promotion of breast feeding, but also by ensuring the proper use of breast-milk substitutes 'when these are necessary' and through 'appropriate marketing'. The Code says that, in the developing world, breast-milk substitutes should not be promoted directly to the consumer, but through the medical profession. Nestlé immediately announced its support for the principles and aim of the Code, and a year later set up the independent Nestlé Infant Formula Audit Commission, chaired by former US Senator and Secretary of State Edmund Muskie. The boycott was lifted in 1984, and in 1991, the commission reached the conclusion that its mandate – to advise the company on its implementation of the WHO International Code of Marketing of Breast-Milk Substitutes – had been achieved, and it was formally dissolved.

Nestlé infant formula marketing policies have been persistently mis-represented by groups and individuals, and have led to attempts in several countries to re-launch boycott action. We would like to set the record straight. Below is our policy for marketing infant formula as it applies in developing countries.

Nestlé:

DOES encourage and support exclusive breast-feeding as the the best choice for babies during the first months of life.

DOES warn mothers of the consequences of incorrect or inappropriate use of infant formula

DOES believe that there is a legitimate market for infant formula when a safe alternative to breast milk is needed

DOES believe that parents have the right to choose how their babies are to be fed on the basis of adequate and objective information

DOES comply with both the letter and the spirit of the World Health Organization's International Code of Marketing of Breast-Milk Substitutes

DOES support efforts by governments to implement the International Code through legislation, regulation or other appropriate measures

DOES encourage sustained breast-feeding after the introduction of complementary foods

DOES NOT advertise infant formula to the public in developing countries

DOES NOT permit its staff to make direct contact with mothers except in response to consumer complaints

DOES NOT give incentives to its staff based on infant formula sales

DOES NOT use pictures of babies on its infant formula packs

DOES NOT distribute free infant formula samples to mothers

DOES NOT give financial or material incentives to health care professionals for the purpose of promoting infant formula

DOES NOT allow educational material relating to the use of infant formula to be displayed publicly in hospitals and clinics

DOES NOT donate free infant formula for use by healthy newborn babies except in exceptional social cases (e.g. where government policy allows manufacturers to respond to a specific medical request, such as if the mother dies in childbirth)

WILL take disciplinary measures against any Nestlé personnel or distributor who deliberately violates this policy.

COMMENTARY

Baby Milk Action have put Nestlé on the back foot. Their campaign against one of their products has forced the company to give a detailed account of its policy. The company has to defend its reputation.

Despite the fact that Baby Milk Action is proactive and uses strong terms: 'aggressively promote', 'condemned', 'diarrhoea', 'death', '4000 babies die' and the final punch line: 'But Nestlé know that if they don't get babies on the bottle, they don't do business'.

Notice though the caution expressed by modifiers: often, likely and modal verbs such as can (twice).

The Nestlé counter argument is very emphatic: notice the sequence of 'Does' and 'Does not' and the final 'Will'. Very significantly though, the two organisations have very different names for the controversial product: Baby Milk and Infant Formula. The Nestlé bulletin makes no acknowledgement at all of the existence of Baby Milk Action.

The argument is not resolved but there is a distinct impression of juggernaut power behind the one and dogged persistence behind the other.

This series of texts ends with a look at an organisation that isn't a business but is a collection of modern heroes, and at a personally motivated campaign arising from tragic circumstances. Amnesty International is concerned with violence abroad and global citizenship in the cause of human rights, the more personal campaign focuses on violent crime on the streets of Britain.

ACTIVITY 60

Torture and murder

The texts below form a leaflet published by Amnesty International. It is part of Amnesty's campaign to seek out those unjustly and brutally deprived of their liberty.

Read the leaflet and identify the different language resources used to give the text an impact.

TEXT 56

"I thought I would never get out of prison. I lost all reason for living." *Vera Chirwa*

On Christmas Eve 1981 Vera and Orton Chirwa were ambushed on a Zambian road. Vera was dragged from the car and knocked unconscious. When she woke up she was in Malawi's notorious Zomba prison.

Vera spent the next 12 years in jail. Her only "crime" was to hold a different opinion to Malawi's then Life-President Dr Hastings Kamuzu Banda.

Although Orton was held in the same prison, they were kept apart, often chained and entirely alone. She was allowed no visitors and no news of her children.

Then in 1988 a fellow prisoner told her that Amnesty International had been campaigning for her release for some years. "This news" she says "brought new hope".

In 1992 a delegation of British lawyers was allowed to visit the prisoners. It was the first time Orton and Vera had been together in 11 years. It would also be the last time. After years of harsh prison life, Orton died just one month later. Vera was not even allowed to attend his funeral.

With Orton's death Amnesty International stepped up its campaign and on January 24th, 1993 Vera was finally pardoned and released. She had become Africa's longest serving Prisoner of Conscience.

Today she is still in Malawi campaigning for human rights.

"I shall never be able to thank Amnesty International enough for fighting for Orton and myself. I shall be indebted to all of you for the rest of my life." *Vera Chirwa.*

You're filth
You're worthless
You're Scum
But you are not forgotten.

Not nice is it. Being called names. No matter what anyone says, words can hurt.

When those words are accompanied by beatings, electric shocks, burns, hammer blows, rape... they become even more painful. Because they start to ring true. Maybe your life really is worth nothing. Maybe nobody cares. Maybe you have been forgotten.

There are thousands of people around the world who live with this daily fear. They are abused, verbally, physically, mentally in the most horrific ways imaginable. But nothing is more terrifying than the thought that they might be forgotten.

Amnesty International exists to make sure that never happens. Every year we take on the cases of more and more innocent people. People who have been locked up simply for the views they hold. The beliefs they stand by. For their sex, or the colour of their skin. We let both them, and their captors, know that they are remembered.

In the short term this alone can mean the difference between life and death.

In the long term we campaign ceaselessly for their release. Since 1961 we have taken on over 43,500 cases. Today thousands of freed ex-prisoners are living proof of the effectiveness of Amnesty International's work.

But we need to do more. And to do that we need your help. Every year we are uncovering the most shocking cases of human rights abuse. You can help us fight these terrible injustices by filling in the form below.

The success of our work depends on people like you. By joining us or making a donation you will become a part of the world's most effective campaign for human rights.

Please do it today. And make sure the world's innocent prisoners are never forgotten.

COMMENTARY

You are considering here texts far removed from supermarkets and ethical business, about people far removed from everyday life in modern Britain.

Notice the point about hurtful names and the insults addressed to unknown second persons. The woman and the child are unknown to the reader who is left wondering what has happened to them. Vera and Orton Chirwa on the other hand have real identities and Vera Chirwa's voice speaks directly in the text. Thus, the voices of the tormentors and the tormented are included.

The appeal at the end is very definitely for money. Note that 'to maintain ... impartiality' Amnesty 'neither seek nor accept money from any government'. Here is an organisation with extraordinary moral force but constantly in need of financial power.

Text 57 is an example of corporate citizenship (The Body Shop) working hand-in-hand with Amnesty to provoke direct action.

TEXT 57

U Pa Pa Lay and U Lu Zaw are traditional Myanmar (Burmese) comedians. At a performance for 2,000 members of the opposition party, the two men sang songs about the country's ruling generals, satirised the military regime and told jokes about state corruption.

Three days later, they were arrested and charged with "spreading false news, knowing it was untrue". Denied legal representation at their trial, both men were sentenced to seven years in jail and sent to a labour camp where they were forced to work with iron bars on their legs. They have since been moved to a prison.

What is happening to U Pa Pa Lay and U Lu Zaw violates Articles 18 and 19 of the Universal Declaration of Human Rights which guarantee freedom of thought and expression.

Both men are Prisoners of Conscience. They have been denied their rights under Article 3, the right to liberty; Article 9, freedom from arbitrary arrest; and Article 8, the right to remedy by a competent authority.

There are three things you can do to defend U Pa Pa Lay and U Lu Zaw:

- you can sign and send the attached pre-written postcard to the Myanmar (Burmese) Embassy
- you can check out Amnesty International's web site. www.amnesty.org.uk
- you can write a letter to General Than Shwe calling for their release:

General Than Shwe
Chairman
State Peace and Development Council
C/O Ministry of Defence
Signal Pagoda Road
Yangon
Union of Myanmar

ACTIVITY 61

A moral crusade

Finally, look at the news report in the *Guardian* of a campaign against violence by Mrs Frances Lawrence, wife of a headteacher murdered by youths. The main question here is how have Ewen MacAskill and John Carvel contextualised the story?

TEXT 58

Moral crusade gathers pace

Parties sign up to manifesto of civic values

Ewen MacAskill and John Carvel

The Conservatives, Labour and Liberal Democrats began a stampede yesterday to claim they were closest to the moral agenda for the regeneration of Britain set out by the widow of Philip Lawrence, the murdered headteacher.

On a day which saw politics, morality and religion mixing unhappily together, the parties vied with one another to lead Frances Lawrence's national movement to renew civic values among Britain's young.

The Conservatives insisted that while Labour spoke about filling the moral vacuum, the Government was putting into place education and law and order measures to meet Mrs Lawrence's concerns. Many of them will be central to tomorrow's Queen's Speech, a Central Office spokesman said.

She had spoken with the Prime Minister and Cabinet colleagues including Michael Howard, the Home Secretary, who said the Government intended to set up a good citizenship award in Mr Lawrence's name.

Labour claimed Tony Blair had been espousing many of the views on civic regeneration before he became leader, and that many of Mrs Lawrence's education plans had been included in a document produced by the shadow education secretary, David Blunkett, last December.

In her "manifesto" Mrs Lawrence called for:

□ A nationwide movement to banish violence and encourage civic values;
□ A ban on the sale of combat knives;
□ New, primary school courses in good citizenship;
□ A higher status in society for teachers and the police;
□ Governments to end neutrality on the concept of the family;
□ Children to be involved in family life, not leading separate lives within the home;
□ An emphasis in teaching on effort, earnestness and excellence.

Differences emerged on the issue of knives. Labour is committed to a ban on knives but the Conservatives said such a ban was difficult as it would affect kitchen knives and Stanley knives.

Mrs Lawrence said simply: "Today is a time for other people to speak. I have nothing further to say at the moment."

Gillian Shephard, Education Secretary, denied that public opinion was driving the politicians into action. Schoolchildren nationwide could have lessons in morality, good citizenship and obeying the law, she indicated.

For Labour, Mr Blunkett said: "Our party's intention is to build on the examples of excellence in personal and social education to ensure that the teaching of citizenship is central to the development of young people from the earliest appropriate moment."

Liberal Democrat home affairs spokesman Alex Carlile warned against being patronising to young people and his colleague Charles Kennedy warned that the action taken by Mrs Lawrence and the Dunblane parents was a comment on the Government.

But the chorus of support from the politicians provoked scepticism from the leader of Britain's second largest teaching union.

Nigel de Gruchy, general secretary of the National Association of Schoolmasters/Union of Women Teachers, said teachers wanted urgent action to crack down on indiscipline in schools instead of moralising from political leaders.

"Teachers have had enough of endless discussions with parents over violent and disruptive youngsters," he said.

Doug McAvoy, general secretary of the National Union of Teachers, said Mrs Lawrence's campaign would be welcomed by teachers and parents who had never believed Mrs Thatcher's edict that "society does not exist".

COMMENTARY

A central feature of the news story is Mrs Lawrence's manifesto call 'to banish violence and encourage civic values'. The writers identify an alternative set of civic values, the reasons for their renewal and the responses of different bodies of opinion. The headline speaks of a 'moral crusade' while the article implies a moral decay in Britain which only Mrs Lawrence seems to be doing anything about. The image of political parties 'beginning a stampede ... to claim they were closest to the moral agenda for regeneration of Britain set out by Mrs Lawrence' is not a flattering one.

The attention of the media was important to Mrs Lawrence as it gave added power as well as publicity to her campaign. Note how she is described in the superscript as 'Murdered headteacher's widow'.

It is interesting that the writers pick up a difference of modality in the views of the then Conservative government and the Labour party. Mr Blunkett expresses intention 'to build on the examples of excellence', whereas Mrs Shephard expresses that, possibility, schoolchildren 'could have lessons in morality'.

Whatever politicians may or may not have been doing, the writers have highlighted Mrs Lawrence's initiative. Just as the opening paragraph, as ever in this kind of discourse, contrasts ineffective political action with a citizen doing something about the problem, so the last paragraph expresses a distinct attitude. it gives the last word to the teachers in the voice of Doug McAvoy, representing a teachers' trade union and denying Mrs Thatcher's edict that 'society does not exist'.

A kind of summary

A word that strikes a more personal note than citizenship is identity. JS, in Auden's poem was certainly a citizen, albeit a passive one, but there is little if anything to show of his identity.

In their album, *Urban Hymns*, The Verve sing *Bitter Sweet Symphony* which has the line:

'But I'm a million different people from one day to the next. I can change.'

It is almost as if modern citizens live in a hall of mirrors, each mirror reflecting a different image or identity. Nearly all the texts in this book offer their readers a different identity, a different role to play. Critical language awareness is a matter of being able to recognise forces that shape the ways we think by the language they use. The issues of identity, power and language have become very big issues indeed. Instead of summarising this chapter in the usual way, we suggest that you re-read the survey at the beginning and then turn to the text below and ask yourself how far the views expressed are reflected in the various kinds of discourse you have been investigating. The text is an abridgement of the *Observer Essay* for 1995, written by Anthony Giddens, Director of the London School of Economics and Political Science (LSE).

TEXT 59

Government's last gasp

The global web of corporate power has released forces beyond national government's control. Is capitalism causing the withering of the state? We live in a time of endings, or so it seems. The end of a millennium, the end of socialism, the end of work, the end of ideology, even the end of history.

These endings have recently been joined by two more, widely proclaimed by pundits – the end of government and of politics. Many think governments have lost the power to govern and political leaders the power to lead.

What are the forces acting to de-stabilise government? One main source is a bubbling diversity of change taking place below the level of the nation state, which is not led by governments, though they must respond to it. Consider the debate about 'family values'. The family has become a hot topic because of human factors, not government initiatives. Women are now laying claim to far more autonomy, inside and outside the home, than they ever had before. Changes are also taking place in 'sub-politics' as people pursue new interests and bring pressure to bear. We are due in the next few years to see many other groups at work besides those that block the construction of new motorways, splash paint on new cars, and try to free calves from the trucks taking them to slaughter.

To sub-politics, we must add huge international changes – 24 hour global money markets, new communications technology and ever larger business corporations, releasing forces with which national governments struggle to cope.

The state is withering and global business is taking charge. Globalisation, we should remember, is about relationships between the small and the large, in which each influences the other. Sub-politics provides a means of thinking about some of the issues involved. The fact that the large corporations are nowhere and everywhere is their strength but also their weakness. Greenpeace meets Shell is not just a case of David and Goliath. It is also a step on the way to reshaping political activity in an era of global change.

6 Reader Power and A-Level English Language

Coursework

The texts you have looked at in this book are a drop in the ocean of texts from which you could select your own examples. You could, for example, choose a supermarket and collect texts in which they enter into a discourse with their customers. In turn, these could be compared with texts produced by another supermarket.

Alternatively, the public relations documents of hospitals, schools, housing departments or of charities such as Age Concern, Oxfam, Save The Children and Mencap, are all rich sources for investigating the ideas that motivate people to do what they do and to communicate in the way that they do.

The way in which issues are reported, set up and debated in newspapers is also a very suitable area for investigative coursework. But you can also use interview techniques to find out what people really think and what words they use for thinking with. Finding out which adverts or statements people judge to be credible, not credible and possibly credible is yet another way of identifying the attitudes and ideas that motivate people, their ideologies.

The way in which Princess Diana has been socially constructed in the minds of millions of people who have never met her is another topic in which a study of discourse in the media can be compared with people's spontaneous thoughts. Is the land mines issue, for example, another instance of what Giddons calls 'sub-political' action or is it big politics? Certainly there is enough press coverage to provide linguistic evidence of attitudes, ideologies and good old fashioned persuasion.

Examinations

An awareness of the wider social, economic and political contexts of non-fiction texts, and of the accumulated historical meanings embedded in words offers additional questions you can ask when analysing a previously unseen text in an examination. Without an understanding of the kind of discourse you are looking at, there is a danger that your analysis will be little more than feature spotting. This does not mean that you should be asking power and language questions of every text you encounter, but that you should be aware of what kind of discourse you have been drawn into. You need to show the examiners your awareness that the text now lying on the operating table, had a social life of its own before being caught and put on an examination paper. The text isn't there merely as a vehicle to test you – it is there as an example of language in use. The key skill, as ever, is to be able to connect the social life of a text to its language bits; which brings us back to stylistics.

Stylistics

Stylistics is a tool rather than an end in itself. You read for entertainment, instruction, information, to engage in argument (persuasive or otherwise), not for stylistics. Thankfully, the repertoire isn't so huge though it may seem so when you first start. You could look at it as a set of choices, conscious and unconscious, which writers make and which readers re-activate the moment they start reading.

Word choices may be looked at semantically: the field they create; whether they are literal or metaphorical, abstract or concrete; formal or less formal choices; whether paired or contrasted, accumulative or isolated; the lexical density of the text contrasted with the use of grammatical words; unusual meanings and inventions.

Word choices will be determined by grammatical choices: pronoun reference; abstract noun phrases; addition of modal verbs; verb agency (who did what?); passivisation (who had it done unto them); connectors and cohesion (joined up thinking words – the 'if's and 'but's and the deictic references such as 'this' and 'that').

The moment you ask questions about verb choices and type frequencies (eg stative and dynamic) you are relating your knowledge of grammar to your knowledge of semantics (making meanings implicitly and explicitly). Descriptions of style also need to take into account, as appropriate, sentence length, function, variation and their overall shape, including how they begin.

With a stylistics repertoire along these lines you are in a position to locate specific linguistic features of a discourse and to begin to decode the implicit meanings and underlying ideology.

Discourse

The aim of discourse investigation is to understand our own thinking better and the way the social world shapes it. Discourse requires an addressee and you, the reader are the other half of the discourse. Being a reader is not unlike being a citizen. In both spheres you can lose your identity or assert it. One way of asserting it, for example, is to identify the role a text assigns to you, or the attitude it expects, and to decide whether or not you accept that role or share that attitude.

Investigating discourse and applying stylistics to written texts is what critical literacy or (critical language awareness) is all about. In this book we have concentrated on reading; it needs another book to focus on critical listening and the exercise of power through the spoken word.

Further reading

Below is a small selection of books that discuss issues of language, power, discourse and ideology. The first two are practical in approach, offering you texts to investigate. The others are important theoretical contributions.

The Language of Newspapers, D. Reah (Routledge, 1998)

The Language of Advertising, A. Goddard (Routledge, 1998)

Literacy in Society, ed R. Hasan and G. Williams (Longman, 1996) esp Chapters 1, 5, 9, 10 and 11.

Language, Ideology and Point of View, P. Simpson (Routledge 1993)

Language as Ideology, R. Hodge and G. Kress, 2nd edition (Routledge, 1993)

Feminist Stylistics, S. Mills (Routledge, 1995)

Language and Power, N. Fairclough (Longman, 1988)

Seeing Through Language: A Guide to Styles of English Writing, R. Carter and W. Nash (Blackwell, 1990)

Introducing Discourse Analysis, D. Nunan (Penguin, 1994)

Sociology, A. Giddens (Polity Press, 1993)

Further reading